LOCAL LAW

IN

MASSACHUSETTS AND CONNECTICUT,

HISTORICALLY CONSIDERED.

BY

WILLIAM CHAUNCEY FOWLER, LL.D.

PREPARED FROM THE NEW ENGLAND HISTORICAL AND GENEALOGICAL REGISTER, WITH ADDITIONS.

ALBANY:
JOEL MUNSELL.
1872.

PREFACE.

The annals of Massachusetts and of Connecticut show that each of these commonwealths have been ever ready to maintain the right of local self-government. The rights granted in charters by the British Crown, in one era, and the rights reserved to the states in the Federal Constitution, in another era, were dearly prized by each commonwealth, as the basis of its local laws.

This love of local law, and the struggles to maintain it, are, in the following pages, set forth in a series of historical facts, in the hope that they would furnish lessons of wisdom for political students of this and future times. A like induction of facts from the annals of other states, of the *Old Thirteen*, would show that they too were animated by the same spirit to struggle for the same object.

Nor is there now any reason for the decay of that spirit, or the cessation of those struggles. After the states had ceased to be colonies, and had formed their own separate Constitutions, they proceeded in due time unitedly to form the present Federal Constitution, as supplementary to the State Constitutions. They so adjusted the Federal Constitution to the State Constitutions, that under a two-fold government the internal concerns of each state could be taken care of by local laws enacted by itself, while the external concerns of the whole could be taken care of by federal laws enacted by the states in congress assembled. Thus the states are separated as to one class of interests, and united as to another class. Thus too, as separated, the states, each of them, can pass such local laws as it sees fit, within the limits of its reserved rights; and the states, as united, can pass such federal laws as they see fit, within the limits of their delegated powers. Under this two-fold government, with two sets of laws, with two sets of agents, the problem is to keep each state government on its own domain within the limits of its reserved rights, and to keep the federal government on its own domain within the limits of its delegated powers. If this problem shall not be worked out, our two-fold government may become the worst government on earth. If it shall be worked out, according to the original idea of the founders of the smaller republics, the separate states, and of the larger federal republic, the United States, it may become the best government on earth.

W. C. F.

DURHAM, CONN., 1872.

LOCAL LAW IN MASSACHUSETTS.

Local law is a relative term. It stands contrasted with imperial law. As used in this paper, it means the laws of the town as distinguished from the laws of the colony or state. Moreover, it means the laws of the colony or state as distinguished from the laws of Great Britain or of the United States.

Plymouth Colony.— The Residence in Holland.

In 1608 a company of English separatists left their native country by stealth, to dwell in Amsterdam. Why did they leave the fruitful fields which they had cultivated, to dwell in a commercial city, inhabited by a strange people, speaking a strange language, and engaged in business foreign to their own? Because, as separatists from the Church of England they had felt or feared the pains and penalties of the imperial laws enacted by the British parliament. After residing in that city, where their religious opinions were tolerated for perhaps a year, why did they with their pastor, John Robinson, and their teaching elder, William Brewster, remove to Leyden? Because there were violent feuds between two other congregations of separatists, which threatened to embarrass them in their self-government as a church. After staying in Leyden about eleven years, why did they leave that "pleasant city," to brave the dangers of the ocean and to dwell in the wilderness exposed to savages? Because they could not practically carry out their principles of self-government as a church, and transmit them to their posterity, among a people to whom they were in danger of becoming assimilated, so that their children, instead of being English, would become Dutch. To preserve their nationality, their language, and their cherished form of church government, they must leave Leyden.

After they had come to this resolution, "the world was all before them where to choose." Guiana, described in the glowing language of Sir Walter Raleigh, as an earthly paradise, was proposed to them. This locality they rejected, because it would expose them to the interference of the jealous and fiery Roman Catholic Spaniard, from whom Leyden had lately suffered so much. Zealand in Holland was proposed to them. But Holland was no longer acceptable as a place of residence. They cast their eyes across the broad Atlantic upon the new world. Here was the soil, here was "ample room and verge enough," where the germs of their civil and religious institutions could take root and expand fully without repression. They were "well inclined" to cross the ocean and take up their home in the colony of New Netherland, on the island of Manhattan, under the protection of the Prince of Orange and the High and Mighty Lords the States General. But this inclination on their part, though encouraged by the directors of the New Netherland company, was not destined to be gratified.

Extract from the Petition of the Directors of the New Netherland Company.

[From the original in the Royal Archives at the Hague; File entitled Admiraliteit.]

Dated February 12, 1620.

"To the Prince of Orange, etc.

"Now it happens, that there is residing at Leyden a certain English Preacher, versed in the Dutch language, who is well inclined to proceed thither to live, assuring the petitioners that he has the means of inducing over four hundred families to accompany him thither, both out of this country and England, provided they would be guarded and preserved from all violence on the part of other potentates, by the authority and under the protection of your Princely Excellency and the High and Mighty Lords States General, in the propagation of the true, pure Christian religion, in the instruction of the Indians in that country in true learning, and in converting them to the Christian Faith, and thus through the mercy of the Lord, to the greater glory of this country's government, to plant there a new Commonwealth, all under the order and command of your Princely Excellency and the High and Mighty Lords States General."

RESOLUTION OF THE STATES GENERAL ON THE PETITION OF THE NEW NETHERLAND COMPANY.

[From the Register of Resolutions of the States General, in the Royal Archives at the Hague.]

"The petition of the Directors of the New Netherland Company, that they, for the peopling of said Island, may be assisted with two ships of war, is rejected."

In the Petition from which the above is taken application is made for two ships. In the refusal to grant the petition for the two ships no notice is taken of the four hundred English families whom the Preacher at Leyden, John Robinson, offered to conduct to America under patronage of the States General. The inference is that the States General did not wish to take them under their patronage.—*New York Colonial History*, vol. I, pp. 24, 25.

A portion of them were in favor of settling with the English planters in Virginia. But it was replied by the others,

"If they should live with the English (Episcopalians) there planted, and under their government, they would be in as great danger to be persecuted for the cause of religion, as if they lived in England, and it might be worse."

Thus there seems to have been some repulsion between themselves and others. They were Aryan in race, but they were Semitic of the Hebrew type, in their proclivity to isolation. On the whole it was, in the language of Bradford, decided "to live in a distinct body by themselves," under the patent of the Virginia company in London; and by their agents to sue his majesty to grant them "free liberty and freedom of religion." From these facts we learn what was the ruling desire in their hearts. It was that they might be in a place where they might have full power to make their own laws. They did not want English laws, or Dutch laws, or Virginia laws, but their own laws.

So intent were they upon obtaining this "free liberty, and freedom in religion," or, in other words, the power to make and enjoy their local laws as separatists in religion, and as separatists in civil polity, that they sent to the great council of England, by their agents, Robert Cushman and John Carver, seven articles adopted by the Leyden church, in which they make large concessions to the church of England, and to the king.

ARTICLES FROM THE CHURCH OF LEYDEN.—1617.

Seven Artikes which ye Church of Leyden sent to ye Counsell of England to bee considered of in respeckt of their judgments occationed about theer going to Virginia Anno 1618.

1. To ye confession of fayth published in ye name of ye Church of England & to every artikell thereof wee do wth ye reformed churches wheer wee live & also els where assent wholy.

2. As wee do acknolidg ye docktrine of fayth theer tawgth so do wee ye fruites and effeckts of ye same docktryne to ye begetting of saving fayth in thousands in ye land (conformistes & reformistes) as ye ar called wth whom also as wth our bretheren wee do desyer to keepe speritual communion in peace and will pracktis in our parts all lawful thinges.

3. The King's Majesty wee acknolidg for Supreame Governor in his Dominion in all causes and over all parsons, and y^{t} none maye decklyne or apeale from his authority or judgment in any cause whatsoever, but y^{t} in all thinges obedience is dewe unto him, either active, if ye thing commanded be not agaynst God's woord, or passive yf itt bee, except pardon can bee obtayned.

4. Wee judg itt lawfull for his Majesty to apoynt bishops, civill overseers, or officers in awthoryty onder hime, in ye severall provinces, dioses, congregations or parrishes to oversee ye Churches and governe them civilly according to ye Lawes of ye Land, untto whom ye ar in all thinges to geve an account & by them to bee ordered according to Godlynes.

5. The authoryty of ye present bishops in ye Land wee do acknolidg so far forth as ye same is indeed derived from his Majesty untto them and as ye proseed in his name, whom wee will also theerein honor in all things and hime in them.

6. Wee beleeve y^{t} no sinod, classes, convocation or assembly of Ecclesiasticall Officers hath any power or awthoryty att all but as ye same by ye Majestraet given unto them.

7. Lastly, wee desyer to geve untto all Superiors dew honnor to preserve ye unity of ye speritt wth all y^{t} feare God, to have peace wth all men what in us lyeth and wheerein wee err to bee instructed by any. Subscribed by

JOHN ROBINSON,
and
WILLYAM BRUSTER.

THE CONCESSIONS ACCOUNTED FOR.

These concessions are remarkable, coming as they do from men who some twelve years before had fled from England with a deep sense of injury in their souls, and, it may be, with maledictions on their lips. How can they be accounted for? It may be that a fuller acquaintance with the fruits of separatism had inspired them with modesty; or that the excellent and liberal Robinson, their pastor, had softened any severity in their feelings; or that the mellowing influence of time and suffering had made them charitable and catholic. But we can also believe that these large concessions, this language of Christian courtesy respecting the Episcopal church, which they once regarded as their mother, and this language of loyalty towards him whom they still considered as their king, can be accounted for by their strong desire to conciliate the king to grant them "free liberty and liberty of religion," that is, authority to make their own laws for their self government. Their love of local law in civil concerns must have been strengthened, if not originated, in Holland, at that time the freest country in Europe, having a system of local law, adopted it is said in New Netherland or New York when under the government of the States General, and if their pride, or principle, or passion, had kept them during the years of their exile, aloof from the king, they were now, when about to seek a forest home in his uninhabited dominions, willing to present their petition to the king through the privy council, accompanied by these propitiatory articles. But all that they could obtain from the king, James I., after the most diligent "sounding," was an oral promise, that he would "connive at their separatism," and not molest them so long as they gave no public offence. But to allow and tolerate them "under the great seal," he would not consent. With this slender encouragement, and putting their trust not in princes but in providence, they hastened the preparations for the voyage to their expected home in the wilderness.

Letter to Sir Edwin Sandys.

The following letter, dated Dec. 15, 1617, and signed by some of the principal members of the Leyden church, shows their self reliance and their competency to self government.

"We believe and trust the Lord is with us, ... and will graciously prosper our endeavors according to the simplicity of our hearts therein. We are well weaned from the delicate milk of our mother country, and inured to the difficulties of a strange and hard land. The people are, for the body of them, industrious and frugal..... We are knit together in a strict and sacred bond and covenant of the Lord, of the violation whereof we make great conscience, and by virtue whereof we hold ourselves strictly tied to all care of others' good. . . . . . . It is not with us, as with others, whom small things can discourage, or small discontentments cause to wish themselves home again."

Origin of their true Love of Local Law.

From these historical facts we learn how it was that this company of emigrants became the practical advocates of local law. In England, they knew by bitter experience the oppressive tyranny of imperial law, the laws of the national church, and the laws of parliament. In Holland, they had seen with their own eyes the beneficial workings of local law. Thus schooled, they understood that imperial law, under a centralized government, is made by those legislators who do not fully understand the wants and interests of many of the people for whom they legislate; but that local laws are made by the people themselves, for the people themselves, who fully understand their own interests and their own wants. As separatists they believed that every local church is competent to take care of its internal concerns, and they were prepared to believe that towns also are competent to take care of their internal concerns. Thus they were prepared to adopt and illustrate, in due time, the general proposition, that local laws made by the people on the spot for themselves, whether as members of a church or citizens of a town, are more likely to be good and appropriate than imperial laws made by men residing at a distance.

Compact formed on Board the Mayflower.

The Mayflower put to sea from Plymouth, England, September 6, 1620, freighted with one hundred and two passengers, the seed corn for a continent, the future representatives of local law in church and state. On the 9th of November, they sighted Cape Cod, and cast anchor in the roadstead of what is now Provincetown. Here they prepared and signed the celebrated compact in the following words:

"In the name of God, Amen. We whose names are underwritten, the loyal subjects of our dread sovereign lord, King James, by the grace of God king of Great Britain, France and

Ireland, defender of the faith &c. having undertaken for the glory of God and the advancement of the christian faith and honor of our king and country a voyage to plant the first colony on the northern parts of Virginia, do by these presents, solemnly and mutually in the presence of God and one another, covenant and combine ourselves together into a civil body politic, for our better ordering and preservation, and furtherance of the ends aforesaid; and by virtue hereof to enact, constitute and frame such just and equal laws and ordinances, acts and constitutions, and offices, from time to time, as shall be thought most meet and convenient for the general good of the colony, unto which we promise all due submission and obedience.

"In witness whereof we have hereunto subscribed our names, at Cape Cod, the 11th of November, in the year of the reign of our sovereign Lord, King James of England, France and Ireland, the eighteenth, and of Scotland the fifty-fourth. Anno Domini, 1020."

On the same day under this compact or constitution, John Carver was elected governor of the Colony for one year.

In thus combining themselves into a body politic, and choosing a governor, they acted in accordance with their original purpose, as stated in the letter of their pastor, Robinson, addressed to them.

Doctrines of the Compact.

In this compact or constitution we find the central doctrines of the Declaration of Independence, adopted one hundred and fifty-six years afterwards by descendants of those who entered into this compact. In equivalent language interpreted by the subsequent acts of the signers of each we have in both instruments the doctrine, that government is founded on compact; that it derives its just power from the consent of the governed; that the people are competent to understand what are the true ends of government, and to adopt the best means for promoting those ends, by passing just and equal laws. Thus viewed, the first five signers of the compact on board the Mayflower, namely: John Carver, William Bradford, Edward Winslow, Will. Brewster and Isaac Allerton, should be placed on the same high level in the annals of the world as the immortal five who drafted the Declaration of Independence, namely: Thomas Jefferson, John Adams, Benjamin Franklin, Roger Sherman and Robert R. Livingston.

It is remarkable that the signers of the compact made no allusion to parliament, the law-making power of England, but speak as if competent to make their own laws.

These noble men have been called pilgrims. They were more than pilgrims. They were the founders of the free institutions of a sovereign state, and largely of the free institutions of a mighty republic, composed of sovereign states. They were not pilgrims with scallopshell, and crucifix, and staff, and scrip, visiting some venerated shrine. They were no saunterers on a professed pilgrimage to the holy land. These voyagers, "weaned from the delicate milk of their mother country," were strong men and brave men, armed with the shield of faith and the sword of the spirit.

> Illi robur et aes triplex
> Circa pectus erat qui fragilem truci
> Commisit pelago ratem
> Primus.

If this could be said by the Roman poet of the fifty-four heroic voyagers on board the Argo, in search of the golden fleece, with how much more emphasis can it be said of those moral heroes who embarked on board the Mayflower, to find beyond the stormy Atlantic the precious boon, liberty.

True they can be called pilgrims, inasmuch as they were foreigners, whether their home was England or heaven. They were pilgrims in the same sense in which Christian is a pilgrim in the immortal work of Bunyan.

The Landing.

Having landed on Monday, the 11th of December, old style, and the 21st, new style, at a place on Cape Cod bay, afterwards called Plymouth, they here, under the compact of government formed in the cabin of the Mayflower, enacted such laws from time to time, as their exigencies required; by a sovereign act inflicting capital punishment without sending the criminal to England for trial; by sovereign acts declaring and carrying on war; by a sovereign act entering into a treaty or compact in the confederation of 1643, with Massachusetts, Connecticut and New Haven.

Exclusive Jurisdiction Claimed.

In 1636 the following declaration was ordered:

"We the associates of New-Plymouth, coming hither as free-born subjects of the state of England, and endowed with all and singular the privileges belonging to such, being assembled, do ordain that no act, imposition or law or ordinance be made or imposed upon us at the present or to come, but such as shall be made and imposed by consent of the body of associates, or their representatives legally assembled, which is according to the free liberties of the state of England."

In this order, then, is the distinct declaration that the local laws of the colony are paramount to all other laws, those of parliament not excepted.

Moreover, the right of local self government, that is, of making its own laws, which it claimed and exercised in its relation to England, it accorded to each of the towns, each town making and administering its own laws as to its internal concerns under the decisions of its own courts, while each town was represented in the general court of the colony, which legislated on those matters which concerned the whole. Thus each town was a little republic complete in itself for its own purposes, while all the towns confederated with one another formed a larger republic complete in itself for its own purposes.

The New England Confederacy.

In the year 1643 the New England Confederacy was formed between the Massachusetts, Plymouth, Connecticut, "and the government of New Haven and the plantations in combination with it." The league or compact thus entered into was declared to be perpetual, and the united colonies were spoken of as a nation for certain purposes, while each colony remained a nation for other purposes.

This confederation or union, was an act of sovereignty of each of the four parties which formed it, shadowing forth the confederation or union of the thirteen states in 1781, by the adoption of the first federal constitution of the united thirteen states, and also the confederation or union of the same thirteen states, by the adoption of the second or present federal constitution of the United States. In being a party to this compact or constitution,

Plymouth did but carry out the compact or constitution made on board the Mayflower, in which, as a body politic, she declared herself competent to form "laws and constitutions."

The third article of this compact of the "united colonies" provides that each colony, or rather that the plantations or towns of each colony, shall retain power to manage its internal concerns. These are the words:

"It is further agreed, that the plantations which at present are, or which shall be hereafter settled within the limits of the Massachusetts, shall be forever under the Massachusetts, and shall have peculiar jurisdiction, among themselves in all cases as an entire body, and that Plymouth, Connecticut and New-Haven shall each of them have like peculiar jurisdiction and government within their limits."

Here we have in this third article of the federal constitution of 1643 just as distinct if not as full provision made by the united colonies for the preservation of local laws and colony rights, as we have in the ninth and tenth articles of the present federal constitution for the preservation of local laws and state rights.

At a meeting of the commissioners of the united colonies of New England, September, 1644, the commissioners of Massachusetts moved that Massachusetts should have the first place in naming the colonies, as a matter of right in the judgment of the general court, as well as in their own judgment. This claim of right the other commissioners would not allow. Yet out of respect to the government of Massachusetts, they granted that the commissioners of Massachusetts should sign first after the president. To this ambitious claim of Massachusetts to precedence, Plymouth the elder sister modestly yielded.

This same spirit of modesty was shown in a letter written in 1665 by the governor of Plymouth, on the subject of forming a new confederation, after New Haven had been absorbed in Connecticut. "We find not our reason seated in sufficient light to continue confederation with three colonies as we did with four." After giving three solid objections, which reflect on the acts of both Massachusetts and of Connecticut in the confederacy, he goes on to say:

"The truth is, we are the meanest, weakest, least able to stand of ourselves, and little able to contribute any helpfulness to others; and we know it, though none should tell us of it; yet through God's goodness, we have not hitherto given you much trouble, and hope it shall be our study and endeavors, as we are able, to be serviceable to our countrymen, brethren and fellow subjects; and doubt not to find the like from yourselves if needed."

Plymouth annexed to Massachusetts.

Plymouth colony had long been striving in vain for a separate charter according to the original purpose of living in a "distinct body by themselves," and that they might thus live under their own laws. On a certain occasion, when it was proposed to connect the colony with New York, it expressed a preference to be connected with Massachusetts as the lesser of two evils. This was improperly construed by the government of England as a willingness to be connected with Massachusetts. Accordingly in the new charter granted by William and Mary, in 1691, Plymouth was merged in Massachusetts just as New Haven had been merged in Connecticut some thirty years before. However gratifying this arrangement may have been to Massachusetts, the feeling in Plymouth colony may be learned from the following letter dated Nov. 5, 1691, from Mr. Wiswall to Governor Hinckley:

"All the frame of heaven moves upon one axis, and the whole of New England's interest seems designed to be loaded on one bottom, and her particular motions to be concentric to the Massachusetts tropic. You know who are wont to trot after the Bay Horse."

Colony of Massachusetts.

In June, 1628, a company of English emigrants under the auspices of John Endicott arrived at Naumkeag, now Salem, to settle upon a territory granted by the "Council for New England," to six patentees, of whom John Endicott was one. Here they found the remains of a small colony which in 1624 had settled at Cape Ann, now Gloucester, but in despair of success there, had removed to this place.

Under a charter obtained, March, 1629, from Charles I., a government was formed for the colony there, by the company in London, John Endicott being appointed governor of the colony. In June, 1629, the colony was strengthened by the arrival of several hundreds, among whom were Francis Higginson, and Samuel Skelton, ordained ministers of the Church of England, but non-conformists. In June, 1630, a still larger reinforcement arrived with John Winthrop, who had been appointed governor.

SYMPATHY WITH THE EPISCOPAL CHURCH.

It will be recollected that these emigrants, when in England, were non-conformist Episcopalians: puritans, but not separatists. And after their removal to Salem, services were conducted in the Episcopal manner, on the arrival of the second company with Higginson. With so little favor did this second company view the separatists, that Mr. Higginson speaking for them said:

> "We will not say as the separatists are wont to say, on their leaving England, Farewell Babylon! Farewell Rome! But we will say, Farewell dear England! Farewell the Church of God in England, and all the christian friends there! We do not go to New England as separatists from the Church of England; though we cannot but separate from the corruptions in it; but we go to practise the positive part of church reformation, and propagate the gospel in America."

Having said these words in the presence of his children and other passengers whom he had called to the stern of the ship to take their last sight of England at Land's End, he concluded with a fervent prayer for the king, and church, and state in England.

Entirely in harmony with this are the utterances of the third company with Governor Winthrop, when they left England, April, 1630. The following language they address to their "brethren," as they style them, "in and of the Church of England:"

> "We desire you would be pleased to take notice of the principals and body of our company, as those who esteem it our honor to call the Church of England from whom we rise, our dear mother, and cannot part from our native country, where she specially resideth, without much sadness of heart, and many tears in our eyes, ever acknowledging that such hope and part as we have obtained in the common salvation, we have received in her bosom, and sucked in from her breasts: We leave it not, therefore, as loathing that milk wherewith we were nourished there, but blessing God for the parentage and education, as mem-

bers of the same body, shall always rejoice in her good, and unfeignedly grieve for any sorrow that shall ever betide her, and while we have breath, sincerely desire and endeavor the continuance and abundance of her welfare, with the enlargement of her bounds in the knowledge of Christ Jesus."

Indeed so strong was the sympathy felt by the colony in Salem, with the Church of England after the arrival of Mr. Higginson, and so great was their disgust with the separatists, that when it was found that Ralph Smith, who came in the same company with Mr. Higginson, was a separatist minister of the gospel, order was given "that unless he would be conformable to the government, he should not exercise his ministry in the colony." Thus silenced or banished, he went first to Nantasket, and then to Plymouth, where he was pastor among the separatists there for six years.

First Ordination in the Colony.

With these facts in mind, the following statements can be appreciated. Within four weeks after the arrival of the company in which were Messrs. Higginson and Skelton, on a day, July 20th, appointed for the choice of a pastor and teacher, before the formation of a church in Salem, the last of these was appointed pastor, and the first was ordained teacher, the last by the laying on of hands of the first, and also three or four grave men, and the first by the laying on of hands of the last and of three or four grave men.

After this, on August 6th, Mr. Higginson having drawn up a church covenant, and thirty persons having assented to it and thus formed themselves into a church, Mr. Samuel Skelton and Mr. Francis Higginson were ordained to the offices of pastor and teacher by the laying on of hands of some of the brethren deputed by the church.

It is to be noted that these two clergymen were ordained, first by the church of England, next by each other assisted by three or four grave men, and thirdly by the church, after that was formed by assenting to the covenant.

In the covenant prepared by Mr. Higginson, the service of the Episcopal Church, which had hitherto been performed, was omitted, much to the dissatisfaction of some of the colonists, among whom were John Brown, a lawyer, and Samuel Brown, a merchant, both in high repute, both members of the council in London, to which the colony was responsible. When these respectable gentlemen expressed themselves strongly on the subject of the omission, Governor Endicott told them that "New England was no place for them," and by the return of the ships sent them back to England.

Why was Ralph Smith banished? Because he would not as a separatist "conform" to the government of the colony and respect their local laws. Why were the Browns banished? Because as Episcopalians they did not respect their local laws. Why were Skelton and Higginson, ordained ministers of the Church of England, reordained, and why did the church of Salem suddenly become a church of separatists? Because the colony determined to throw off all subordination to the English Church, and place themselves under their own local laws. The filial feelings which rose up in their hearts and overflowed at their eyes as they looked upon the green fields of their country, and upon the churches and cathedrals where they had worshipped, gave place to a desire for independence, in church and state. Political independence could more easily be obtained by cutting all connection with the English national Church. We cannot believe they wore a mask when they left England and cast it off when they came to Salem. We do not mean to approve or condemn their conduct, but to account for it.

Transfer of the Charter.

Having settled the basis of their church estate, they next proceeded to settle the basis of civil government. The first charter of Massachusetts, dated March 4th, 1628, and bearing the signature and seal of Charles the First, was, in form, like other charters given to companies resident in England. In the language of Judge Story, the whole structure of the charter presupposes the residence of the company in England, and that they will transact their business there. There was in it no authority from the king to transfer the charter and the government to New England. And yet in 1629, they assumed the right to transfer the charter and the government to New England, though they evidently did this with some fears and some misgivings, "carrying the business secretly that the same be not divulged." Afterwards they boldly transferred the charter from the place where it belongĕd, to the place where the colonists wanted it to be, without asking consent of the king.

Why was this bold, yet secret transfer of the charter made? It was made because so long as the charter continued in England, the government of the colony must be vested in the company there; but when it was transferred to Massachusetts, the government would be vested in the colony there, who would thus be able to make their own local laws. By the act of transfer, of which the king had just ground of complaint, the colony of Massachusetts distinctly declared that, as in ecclesiastical, so in political concerns, they would be governed by their own local laws, and not by laws made in England. We do not mean to approve their conduct or to condemn it, but to account for it.

The Right of Suffrage.

As the colony had decided to enact its own laws, they saw it was necessary that good laws should be enacted in order that they should be worthy of obedience and support. And in order that good laws should be enacted, they judged it necessary that they should be enacted by good men. And in order that good men only should act as legislators, they decided to restrict the right of suffrage to members of the church.

Accordingly, in May, 1631, in less than a year after the charter was transferred, at the first general court for election, after the arrival of Governor Winthrop, who had first been elected governor in England, the following act was passed:—

"To the end that the body of the commons may be honest and good men, it was ordered and agreed, that for the time to come, no man shall be admitted to the freedom of this body politic, but such as are members of some of the churches within the limits of the same."

By thus limiting the right of suffrage to the aristocracy of goodness rather than extending it to the democracy at large, they threw the power of the state directly into the hands of the churches, and indirectly into the hands of those who decided who should be church members, namely, the clergy. In this union, thus formed, between church and state, they believed that the moral goodness of the one would be so communicated to the other that all laws would be better than the laws of a centralized government like England.

In May, 1634, the general court adopted the form of an oath which all the freemen were required to take on their admission to the freedom of the body politic. In this oath, each one bound himself "as a subject of the government to maintain all the liberties and privileges of the commonwealth, and to submit himself to all the wholesome laws and orders:" while no mention is made of the laws of England. The general court acted as if entirely independent of England.

Functions of the Towns.

The same attachment to local law which was shown in the relation of the colony to England, was shown also in the relation of the towns to the colony itself. In the records of the general court, 1636, is the following act:—

"Inasmuch as particular towns have many things which concern only themselves, and the ordering of their own affairs, and disposing of their own towns, it was ordered that the freemen of every town or the major part of them, shall only have power to dispose of their own lands and woods, with all the privileges and appurtenances of said towns not repugnant to the laws and orders established by the general court," &c.

In the functions of the towns stated in this act and elsewhere, there are virtually the three branches of a system of government, the legislative, the judicial and the executive. Called from time to time to act in making laws for the town, laws affecting their own rights and interests, the inexperienced yeomanry of those times found themselves in a school, in which the elementary principles of government were practically taught. Having become acquainted with these principles they would, some of them, be sent by their townsmen to the general court to make laws for the colony. Thus the leading men of the town, making the laws for the town with others, and making with others the laws of the colony, would understand the value of the local laws of the town, in its relation to the colony, and the local laws of the colony in its relation to England. And what a part thus acquired would soon be the property of the whole. Thus each town was a body politic, acting first as an independent republic in the management of its internal concerns, and second, as a member of a confederated republic, in sending its delegates to the general court of the colony.

The Banishment of Roger Williams.

This remarkable man arrived in Massachusetts in 1631, and after acting as a religious teacher in Salem, and for a period afterwards at Plymouth, and then returning to Salem, was banished in 1635, by the magistrates and general court, from the colony.

As he was a man of education, great moral worth, and supremely devoted to religion, and may be considered the founder of Rhode Island; the inquiry naturally comes up for an answer: Why did the general court banish Roger Williams? The answer to that question may be found in the following statement, contained in the order of the general court. "Sept. 3d, 1635. Whereas Mr. Roger Williams, one of the elders of the church of Salem, hath broached and divulged divers new and dangerous opinions against the authority of magistrates, as also writ letters of defamation both of the magistrates and churches here, and that before any conviction, and yet maintaineth the same without retraction, it is therefore ordered, that the said Mr. Williams shall depart out of this jurisdiction within six weeks now next ensuing; which if he neglect to perform, it shall be lawful for the governor and two of the magistrates to send him to some place out of this jurisdiction, not to return any more without license from the court." With this statement the following declaration of John Cotton agrees.

"Two things there were, which, to my best observation and remembrance, caused the sentence of his banishment, and two others fell in, that hastened it."

As the first of these he specifies Williams's "violent and tumultuous carriage against the patent," the inestimable foundation, as he proceeds to show in some detail, of the privileges and property of the colonists. As the second cause, he names the strictly political one, that "when the magistrates and other members of the general court, upon intelligence of some episcopal and malignant practice against the country, made an order of court to take trial of the fidelity of the people, not by imposing upon them, but by offering to them, an oath of fidelity, that, in case any should refuse to take it, they might not betrust them with place of public charge and command, this oath, when it came abroad, he vehemently withstood it, and dissuaded sundry from it, partly because it was, as he said, Christ's prerogative to have his office established by oath, partly because an oath was a part of God's worship, and God's worship was not to be put upon carnal persons."

The occasions which "hastened" the proceeding against him, Cotton represents to have been Williams's appeal to the churches against the magistrates, and his renouncing communion with the church of Salem on account of its refusal to proceed with him in his disorganizing measures.

We here see, that the head and front of his offending was his opposition to some of the local laws of Massachusetts, which the general court were determined to defend, even by this act of banishment.

The New England Confederacy.

The four young New England colonies severally on Cape Cod bay, Massachusetts bay, Connecticut river and Long Island sound, separated as they were from the mother country, naturally looked to one another for any help they might need. They were one in race, in a common faith, in their common trials, and in their fears of their common enemies, the Indians. But no political bond of union existed between them.

In 1638, the subject of forming a confederacy came before them; but owing to "divers differences" between Massachusetts and Connecticut, the matter was delayed. The former, in her love of power, wanted the "preeminence;" the latter, in her jealousy, showed a "shyness" of coming under the government of the former, from which she had just escaped. She had submitted to the government of Massachusetts one year, and had repudiated it. Moreover, as we learn from Winthrop and Hooker, Massachusetts insisted that the confederation should have power to decide all questions which appropriately came before it, without an appeal to the several general courts, thus inclining to make the confederation a strong government, which by her "preeminence" she might control. Connecticut, on the other hand, insisted that, in case of a want of unanimity in the confederacy, the question at issue should be referred to the several courts for final decision.

In 1643, the confederacy was formed, and two commissioners from each colony held their first meeting. In the articles of compact or constitution, the colonies were to be styled, THE UNITED COLONIES OF NEW ENGLAND; the union was to be perpetual; the vote of six of the eight commissioners was to be final; and questions upon which as many as six could not agree should be referred to the general courts of the several colonies.

In 1645, Connecticut laid an export duty at Saybrook. Massachusetts refused to pay it. Plymouth and New Haven colonies sustained the action of Connecticut. Massachusetts still refused to submit. So dissatisfied was the general court, that it proposed that the articles of confederation should be revised, and that Massachusetts should have one more commissioner than either of the other colonies. Massachusetts was not willing to keep covenant with the other colonies, and be bound by her own compact. And why was this? It was because she wished to have her own laws paramount to the acts of the federal congress of the united colonies. So dissatisfied was she with those acts, that she passed an act of her own, retaliating not only upon Connecticut, but upon the other colonies also. This drew from the commissioners of those colonies a dignified letter of remonstrance addressed to Massachusetts.

In 1653, all the commissioners of the united colonies, except Bradstreet of Massachusetts, voted in favor of war against the Dutch at Manhattan, and Ninigret an Indian chief. As the confederation was formed for "offence and defence," and by the constitution thereof the vote of six commissioners was to be binding upon all the colonies, Massachusetts was bound by covenant to submit to that vote. The house of deputies communicated their resolve to the commissioners: that "they did not understand they were called to make a present war with the Dutch." A committee appointed by the general court, reported it to be a "scandal to religion that a general court of Christians should be obliged to act and engage upon the faith of six delegates against their conscience." The same committee reported that the sixth article of confederation which gives authority to the commissioners "to hear, examine, weigh and determine all affairs of war," relates only to "*defensive* war."

Thus Massachusetts exposed herself to the well grounded charge brought against her by the other colonies, of breaking her covenant with them and of "dissolving the confederacy." It should be added, in justice to Massachusetts, that in September, 1654, she withdrew her false interpretation of the sixth article of the federal constitution of the united colonies. It is remarkable that in both of these cases in which Massachusetts placed her own local laws above the federal constitution of the united colonies, the interests of other colonies were at stake and not her own.

The Coinage of Money.

In 1652, the general court established a mint house and appointed John Hull mint-master, for the coinage of silver pieces of the value of twelvepence, sixpence and threepence, with the same alloy as sterling money, each piece containing three-fourths of the weight of metal in the English pieces of the same denomination. This money and sterling money were declared to be the only legal tender. The pieces are known by the names of the *pine tree* shilling and the *pine tree* sixpence. Thus the colonial legislature assumed the sovereign right to coin money and declare the value thereof. But complaints were made in England against the colony for this act, and a proposal was made in his majesty's name, in 1665, that the law authorizing the coinage of money should be repealed, for which the following reason was given; "For coining money is a royal prerogative." But, notwithstanding this, the mint continued in operation thirty years from the time of its establishment; though it is remarkable that during that period the date 1652 continued on all the pieces, though coined from more than twenty different dies. Massachusetts thus had the boldness to assume the sovereign right to coin money in opposition to the king's authority, and yet by putting on a false date she had the adroitness to escape any penalty, for a time, namely, until she lost her charter. Such was the tenacity with which the colony adhered to its local laws.

Cromwell's Proposals.

In 1653, Oliver Cromwell became Protector of England; and after his conquest of Ireland, he proposed to the people of New

England to take up their abode in that Island. This offer Governor Endicott for Massachusetts courteously declined. He then proposed that the people of New England should remove to Jamaica, which he had recently conquered. This offer the general court also declined. He could offer strong inducements to the puritans, himself a puritan, wielding as he did the power and patronage of the government of England. He declared:

> "That he did apprehend the people of New-England had as clear a call to transport themselves from thence to Jamaica, as they had from England to New-England, in order to their bettering their outward condition, God having promised that his people should be the head and not the tail; besides that design had this tendency to overthrow the man of sin."

If he could thus tempt their ambition, they in their correspondence could address themselves to his vanity by religious compliments. In this diplomacy the puritans in the government of Massachusetts were a full match for the puritan protector of England. They could promise him their prayers, speak of his labors of love to God's people, as overthrowing the enemies of his truth, as enlarging the kingdom of his dear son. But they refused to comply with his wishes that they would remove to Ireland or Jamaica. Why did they not yield to his wishes? Because by so doing they would come into practical subjection to England, and thus lose the privilege of making their own local laws. The colony chose rather to be a puritan commonwealth in Massachusetts, self governed, than to be subject to a puritan commonwealth in England.

Laws against Quakers.

In the years 1656, '57, '58, '59, '60, the general court passed laws against the quakers, prohibiting their residence in the colony. Under these laws they were to be sent to jail, or whipped, or kept at hard work, or to have their tongues bored through with a red-hot iron. Under these laws, quakers were put to death in much the same spirit in which a leading minister of Boston cried out, "I would carry fire in one hand and faggots in the other, to burn all the quakers in the world."

But a quaker named Burroughs gained access to his majesty, King Charles II., and alluding to these punishments in Massachusets, said to him, "There is a vein of blood opened in your dominions which, if not stopped, will overcome all." The good natured monarch replied, "I will stop that vein." "Then do it speedily, for we know not how many may be put to death," said Burroughs. "As speedily as you will; call the secretary, and I will do it presently." The *mandamus* or order was made out, signed by the king, 1662, and forwarded by the quakers to the governor of Massachusetts, by one Shattuck, who had been banished from the colony under penalty of death if he should return.

In Boston, the news of the arrival of the king's messenger and the cry that "Shattuck and the devil had come" spread consternation among the people assembled on the sabbath. When admitted with the ship-master to the presence of Governor Endicott, he was ordered to take off his hat. On receiving the king's *mandamus*, the stout hearted governor restored to him his hat, took off his own, and after consultation said, "we shall obey his majesty's command." In this order the colony was prohibited from inflicting corporal punishment, and required to send quakers obnoxious to punishment by the laws, to England for trial.

The magistrates and the general court did not "obey the commands of the king." Quakers obnoxious to punishment were not sent to England for trial; and some of the quakers after this suffered corporal punishment, by being whipped through the streets, or thrown into prison, or whipped at the cart-tail in three several towns. They valued their own local laws more than the commands of the king, but they sent Mr Norton and Mr. Bradstreet to England to conciliate him.

It should be added that Massachusetts was so intent upon carrying out her own statute laws with respect to the quakers, that in September, 1656, the general court sent a letter, signed by Edward Rawson, to the federal commissioners, complaining of the quakers, and that in consequence two or more of the other colonies passed laws against the quakers, thus sustaining the laws of Massachusetts.

Christmas and the Prayer Book.

In 1659 the general court passed a law:

> "That whosoever should be found observing any such day as Christmas, or the like, either by forbearing to labor, feasting or any other way upon any such account, as aforesaid, every such person so offending, shall for every such offence pay five shillings as a fine to the country."

This colony law was objected to by the king in the year 1665, as "contrary to the laws of England," with the proposal that it should be repealed. But though thus objected to as contrary to the laws of England, and though the charter distinctly provided that all "such laws and ordinances" passed by the colony, be not contrary to the laws and statutes of the realm of England, this law continued on the statute book twenty-two years, until 1681, when it was repealed, perhaps because the charter was in danger. Thus Massachusetts had the boldness to keep the local law "contrary to the laws of England," sixteen years after it had been objected to by the commissioners appointed by the king.

Prior to 1662, the general court passed a law making it penal to use the Common Prayer Book of the Church of England. To this law the royal commissioners objected in 1665:

> "It being scandalous that any person should be debarred the exercise of his religion according to the laws and customs of England, by those who by the indulgence granted have liberty left to be what profession in religion they please."

The general court in their reply refused to change the law.

The Royal Commission.

In April, 1665, five commissioners, of whom Col. Richard Nichols was chairman, were authorized by the king to visit his majesty's colonies in New England, and make report to him or his privy council, from time to time. The commissioners brought with them a letter from the king, Charles II., dated April, 1664, containing instructions to the commissioners, in which mention is made of a letter addressed by the king, June 28, 1662, to the governor of Massachusetts, which had not, it appears, received the attention desired.

The arrival of commissioners, and the presentation of the commission under which they acted, created jealousy and alarm in the colony, which the subsequent course of the commissioners was not calculated to remove. Instead of settling the difficulties between England and themselves with the commissioners appointed for the purpose, the general court addressed to the king a long letter signed by Governor Endicott, in which, in humble language, they beg his favor, but do not comply with his wishes.

After complaining of the commissioners, and claiming the right to make their own laws, and enjoy their "liberties which are far dearer to us than our lives," the letter closes with a paragraph from which the following is taken:

> "Royal Sir — It is in your power to say of your poor people of New-England, they shall not die. If we have found favor in the sight of our king, let our life be given at our petition, or rather that which is dearer than life, that we have ventured our lives (for), and willingly passed through many deaths to obtain, and our all. At our request, let our government live, our patent live, our magistrates live; our laws and liberties live, our enjoyments live; so shall we have further cause to say, from our hearts, let the king live forever."

They made a distinction between loyalty to the person of the king, and obedience to his laws. They could cry, Lord, Lord, but would not do his will. They chose to be governed by their own local laws.

Laws Disallowed by the King's Commissioners.

By the charter granted by Charles the First, March 18, 1628, the colony were allowed to make laws and ordinances,

> "So as such laws and ordinances be not contrary or repugnant to the laws and statutes of this our realm of England."

In May, 1665, the commissioners on examination of the colony statute book reported to the general court twenty-six criticisms or censures upon the laws, and proposed that the general court should amend these laws by alterations or additions, or by repealing them.

The general court, in response to this proposal, were willing to make some alterations in the laws, and actually did make them. But to other laws they adhered with unyielding tenacity. The commissioners therefore departed to England without having accomplished the object of their mission. They had been received and treated so differently, in Massachusetts, from what they had been in Plymouth and Connecticut, that after their return the king addressed to these latter colonies a letter in which is the following commendation:

"And although your carriage doth of itself most justly deserve our praise and approbation, yet it seems to be set off with the more lustre by the contrary deportment of the colony of Massachusetts, as if by their refractoriness they had designed to recommend and heighten the merit of your compliance with our directions for the peaceable and good government of our subjects in those parts."

What was the cause of this treatment of the royal commissioners, on the part of Massachusetts? It was her extreme jealously at any interference with her local laws, even when those laws were "repugnant to the laws" of England, and thus in violation of her charter.

A Douceur offered to the King.

When in 1682 the charter granted by Charles the First was in danger, the general court of the colony, at the suggestion of Cranfield, governor of New Hampshire, instructed their agents in London to wait upon Lord Hyde, and offer him two thousand guineas for the private use of the king, Charles II. This act, though the offer was not accepted, shows how highly the colony valued the charter which was the basis of their laws. The general court would not have stooped to bribery and corruption, unless they expected to secure a valuable consideration for the two thousand guineas, namely the liberty of being governed by their local laws.

The Writ Quo Warranto and Loss of the Charter.

The writ *quo warranto* was issued against the colony, June, 1683, requiring the government thereof to show why they exercised certain powers under the charter. The colony neglected to appear in court by its agents, and so the case went by default, in the loss of the charter. Why the colony neglected to make answer, when summoned by the king, it is difficult to say, unless it was because the rulers and the people were conscious that they could not meet the charges against them of having violated the charter by the assumption of powers it did not confer.

Robert Humphrey, Esq., agent for Massachusetts Bay, in his letter to the governor and council, dated Inner Temple, May, 1685, and read in the general court the 8th of July following, writes:

"The breaches assigned against you are as obvious as unanswerable, in that all the service your council and agent could have done you, would have only served to deplore, not prevent that inevitable loss. I sent you the lord's papers, order of June, 1684, requiring your appearance on the first day of Michaelmas term, else the judgment against your charter was to stand. When the first day came, your letters neither were nor could be returned."

Thus it appears that though the charter of Charles I. was lost by default, it could not have been saved by appearing in court; the colony had so violated the charter that the court must vacate it. In other words, the colony lost the charter from its strong attachment to its local laws.

The history of Massachusetts under the lost charter shows that the colony government, in its disputes with the mother country, insisted: 1. That all their rights granted to them by charter should be enjoyed by the colony to their full extent, according to their own construction of that royal grant. 2. That when they found they could promote their views by exercising powers not granted by the charter, they could be justified in so doing, by the plea of necessity, or of their conscience, or by an appeal to the Bible, interpreted by themselves.

Thus Governor Leverett, 1676, in his interview with a royal commissioner, declared:

"That the laws of England were binding no further than consisted with their interests; that full legislative powers were conferred upon the company; that all matters in dispute were to be considered by their determination without any appeal; and that his majesty ought not to retrench their liberties which he had agreed to confirm and leave them to enjoy, or even enlarge the same."

The colony cared little for the laws of England in comparison with their own laws. For these laws they consented to forfeit the charter, that palladium which they seemed to value as highly as the ancient Trojans did the heaven-descended shield of Pallas.

The Provincial Charter.

The colony had been sometime without a charter, and thus subject entirely to the legislation of England, and to the discretion of the king. All efforts to restore the lost charter must prove abortive. The king had evidently determined to erect a new government, under which the Plymouth colony also should be placed. The first draught of the charter was objected to, by the agents of Massachusetts, because of its limitation of the powers of the governor, who was to be appointed by the king. The second draught was also objected to; whereupon the agents were informed that "they must not consider themselves as lenipotentiaries from a foreign state, and that if they were unwilling to submit to the pleasure of the king, his majesty would settle the country without them, and they might take what would follow."

The new charter granted by William and Mary in 1691 went into operation in 1692. As compared with the old charter granted by Charles I. it abridged the rights of the colony, and was therefore submitted to with reluctance, though accepted by the general court. As under the first charter, so under this, the colony now united with Plymouth endeavored to enlarge its rights and liberties beyond the provisions of the charter.

In 1722, an act was passed by the provincial legislature setting forth that:

"No aid, tax, tollage, assessment, custom, loan, benevolence or imposition should be laid, assessed or levied upon any of his majesty's subjects, or their estates, on any pretence whatsoever but by the act and consent of the governor, council and representatives of the people assembled in general court."

This act, negatived by the king under the charter, shows the animus of Massachusetts in regard to her local laws.

In 1722, seven articles of complaint were brought forward by the British ministry against the house of representatives of the general court, for encroaching on the king's prerogative.

1. Their taking possession of the royal masts and cutting them into logs for sawing.

2. Their refusing the governor's negative on the speaker.

3. Assuming authority without the governor and council to appoint fasts and thanksgivings.

4. Adjourning themselves for more than four days at a time.

5. Dismantling of forts and ordering the guns and stores into the treasurer's custody.

6. Suspending military officers and mulcting them of their pay.

7. Sending a committee of their own to muster the king's forces.

Upon a hearing before the king and council, the provincial agent, Elisha Cook, acknowledged that the house of representatives were guilty in respect to the first, third, fifth, sixth and seventh articles, having been led into the errors by former assemblies. The other two articles were regulated by an explanatory charter, by which the governor had a negative on the election of the speaker, and the house could not adjourn for more than two days. This explanatory charter the house accepted.

Under the charter of 1691, the governor was appointed by the crown, but his salary was paid by the province. For the purpose of enlarging their powers against the royal prerogatives, the house of assemby would often delay voting his salary, or diminish it, in order that they might thus influence him to sign bills to which he was opposed. In order to preserve the independence of the governor, the crown after a time paid his salary. But so jealous was the house of assembly of this act of the crown, and so anxious were they to retain all the colony rights, that it expressed great dissatisfaction. It was not willing that the governor should thus be made independent, to the injury of their local laws, which they valued more than money.

THE PROVINCIAL CHARTER IN DANGER.

The violations of the first charter, granted by Charles I., which caused it to be forfeited, and the violations of the provincial charter, granted by William and Mary, described in the last section, were sufficient to awaken suspicions that the province was aiming at independence. These suspicions amounting to belief, were, in the language of Jeremiah Dummer, an agent of Massachusetts in London, expressed by "people of all conditions and quality." Such people, holding such a belief, would naturally adopt the opinion that the colonies ought to be deprived of their charters, and made entirely subject to the crown.

In contravention of this opinion Mr. Dummer published in 1721 an able defence of the New England charters addressed to Lord Carteret, one of the secretaries of state, in which he declared that the people of Massachusetts as well as of the other colonies, would esteem "the loss of their privileges a greater calamity than if their houses were all in flames at once, the one being a reparable evil, the other irreparable. Burnt houses may rise again out of their ashes, and even more beautiful than before, but 'tis to be feared *that liberty once lost is lost forever.*" While the colony thus shuddered at the thought of losing their charters, the basis of their local laws, so intent were they upon enacting other laws not provided for in the charter, that they exposed themselves to be deprived of that charter.

Taxation and Local Law.

Massachusetts believed that taxation and representation were inseparable; that taxation without representation is tyranny; and that as the colony was not represented in parliament the mother country had no right to impose taxes upon the people of the colony.

"In November, 1703, in answer to the governor's message, the house declared, 'that it had been the privilege from Henry the third, and confirmed by Edward the first, and in all reigns unto this day, granted and now is allowed, to be the just and unquestionable right of the subject, to raise *when* and dispose of *how*, they see cause, any sum of money by consent of parliament; *the which privilege we her majesty's loyal and dutiful subjects here have lived in the enjoyment of*, and do hope always to enjoy the same, under our most gracious Queen Anne and successors, and shall ever endeavor to discharge the duty incumbent on us."

Apprehensive that the British cabinet still contemplated raising money in America, by act of parliament: the general court of Massachusetts, in November, 1755, instructed their agent in London "to oppose anything that should have the remotest tendency to raise a revenue in the plantations, for the public use or services of government.

They were willing to be taxed by local laws enacted by their own legislature in which they were represented, but they were not willing to be taxed by the imperial laws of England enacted by parliament in which they were not represented.

The Relations of the Clergy to Local Law.

In the colony of Massachusetts Bay the right of suffrage was enjoyed only by church members. As the clergy practically had the power to determine who should be members of the church, they thus had the power to determine who should enjoy the right of suffrage and who should make the laws. Thus the clergy virtually, by means of the members of their churches, enacted the laws of the colony, and determined the mode of their administration, or their repeal.

From the letter of Governor Winthrop on the formation of the New England confederacy, and from other facts, we learn that the clergy took an active part in the colonial legislation, especially in that portion of it which related to religious concerns. The clergy were personally and professionally interested to impart such vigor to the local legislation of the colony as should protect them from the interference of the parliament and the bishops. In other words, under the first charter in the ecclesiastical and civil polity of the colony, the general court made the laws, the members of the church made the general court, and the clergy made the members of the church. To the influence of the clergy has been attributed the enactment of those local laws under which Episcopalians, Baptists, Quakers, and other denominations were persecuted. It is remarkable when complaints in the name of the king came against the colony for allowing only members of the puritan churches to vote, the general court was ready, from fear of losing their charter, to extend the right of suffrage to all of a "good moral character;" and yet they professed to give to the clergy the power of determining who had this "good moral character;" thus practically still leaving to the clergy the right to say who should be voters. Thus in the committee appointed by the general court to make a draught of the fundamental laws of the colony, Rev. Hugh Peters, Rev. John Cotton, and Rev. Thomas Shepard, were members. Thus, too, in 1662, Rev. John Norton with Simon Bradstreet, a leading man in the colony, were sent to England on the important mission to settle the difficulties which had arisen between the colony and the mother country.

Thus, too, in 1688, the Rev. Increase Mather was sent to England, where he was instrumental in procuring the provincial charter under which Plymouth and Massachusetts were united.

The puritan clergy of Massachusetts had all that influence throughout the colony which their brethren, the puritan clergy of England, had in their several congregations, as described by Macaulay in his *History of England* by Addison in the 317th number of the *Spectator*, and by Sir John Hawkins in his *Life of Johnson*. This influence they exerted in promoting the enactment of the local laws.

The Relation of their Local Laws to the Bible.

The present version of the Bible authorized by King James was published in 1611. It was read with the greatest enthusiasm by many of the puritans, who regarded it as containing the sum of all earthly and all heavenly wisdom. The puritans of Massachusetts Bay were ready to run a parallel between their own experience and that of the Israelites. They had their own Pharaoh, their own house of bondage, their own sea, their own wilderness, their own Canaanites to contend with, and their own Moses and Aaron. And they were willing to assimilate themselves to the Israelites by adopting a portion of their code of laws.

They did not stop to consider that these laws were made for a peculiar people of a different race, in a different age of the world, and living on a different part of the globe; but they only thought them as made for a chosen people of God by God, the great Legislator. It was afterward found on experience and observation that some of these laws were better adapted to a race like the Hebrews, who were to be kept apart from the rest of the world, than for an Aryan race, like these Anglo-Saxons who were destined to become the "universal Yankee nation."

Stamp Act.

The stamp act was passed by the British parliament in 1765. The measure was defended by Grenville, by the following arguments:

"That this kingdom has the sovereign, the supreme legislative power over America, is granted; it cannot be denied; and taxation is a part of that sovereign power. It is one branch of the legislation. It is, it has been, exercised over those who are not, who never were, represented...... When I proposed to tax America, I asked the house if any gentleman would object to the right. I repeatedly asked it; and no man would attempt to deny it. Protection and obedience are reciprocal. Great Britain protects America: America is bound to yield obedience...... The nation has run itself into an immense debt to give them protection; and now when they are called upon to contribute a small sum toward the public expense, or expense arising from themselves, they renounce your authority, insult your officers, and break out, I might almost say, into open rebellion."

But these arguments did not satisfy the general court and the people of Massachusetts. They stood upon their rights in refusing to pay the stamp duty, as Englishmen under the British constitution. Their declaration was, that taxation without representation is contrary to that constitution, and was therefore tyranny, and ought to be resisted. Parliament called this resistance rebellion; but they believed that an unconstitutional law is null, and that resistance to such a law is obedience to God, and justified by the British constitution.

Such was the opposition to the stamp act, that Oliver, the stamp master, was hung in effigy, and Governor Hutchinson's house was attacked, because he was supposed to be in favor of the act. The stamp act was repealed in 1766. Thus Massachusetts contended successfully for her colonial rights and local laws, in opposition to imperial law.

External Taxes.

In 1767, parliament laid a duty on tea, paper, glass, and other articles, that thus by an external tax, under the conceded right to regulate commerce, it might accomplish what it failed to accomplish by an internal tax under the stamp act. The colony had hitherto submitted to the exaction of an external tax in the shape of a duty on imported goods. But knowing well what was the *animus* of parliament in passing the law, there was the same opposition to it as to the stamp act. "We will," they said, "form an association to eat nothing, drink nothing, wear nothing imported from Great Britain. If our opposition to slavery is called rebellion, let us pursue our duty with firmness, and leave the worst to Heaven." An external tax they regarded as making them slaves if they submitted to it, and hence they resisted it.

When Dr. Franklin, in December, 1774, drew up a plan for settling the difficulties between Great Britain and the colonies, one of the conditions proposed by him, and regarded by Massachusetts as indispensable, was, "that all power of internal legislation should be disclaimed by parliament." This was declared by high British authority to be "inadmissible." Still Massachusetts persistently asserted her right to manage her own internal concerns without the interference of Great Britain. Hutchinson, the royal governor, claimed supremacy for parliament in all cases whatever. This claim Massachusetts resisted, from their strong attachment to their local laws.

The Right of Self Government.

In 1640, Winthrop, page 30, vol. ii, remarks:

"Upon the great liberty which the King had left the Parliament in England, some of our friends then wrote to us advice, to send over some to solicit for us in Parliament, giving us hope that we might obtain much. But consulting about it, we declined the motion for this consideration, that if we should put ourselves under the protection of Parliament, we must then be subject to all such laws as they should make, or at least such as they might impose upon us."

Upon this passage, transcribed for his letter to Baron Van der Capellan, a distinguished Dutch statesman, in 1779, Governor Trumbull, one of the most deliberate assertors of the American revolution, and then custodian of the first two manuscript volumes of this history, remarks:

"Here observe, that, as at this time, so it hath been ever since, that the colonies, so far from acknowledging the parliament to have any right to make laws binding on them in all cases whatsoever, they have denied it in any case."

Chalmers speaks of Massachusetts as "always fertile in projects of independence." "Disregarding equally her charter and the laws of England, Massachusetts established for herself an independent government similar to those of the Grecian republics" (Book I, page 400). It appeared more rational to them (the colonists), that the colony should be governed by those who made it the place of their residence, than by men dwelling at the distance of three thousand miles, over whom they had no control. The object was self government under their own local laws.

Civil Superior to Military Authority.

In 1757, Lord London, in view of a certain act of the general court of Massachusetts, made the declaration that "in time of war the rules and customs of war must govern." This declaration was brought before the general court and condemned in a message which it sent to the governor, in which it declares that "the rules and customs of war were not the rules which the civil magistrate was to govern himself by." Thus Massachusetts took ground against military despotism, and in favor of the supremacy of civil law over military rules and of civil rulers over military despots.

In 1769, the house of representatives, when the governor (appointed by the crown) refused at their request to remove the troops from the town of Boston, declared:

> "That the use of the military power, to enforce the execution of the law, is, in their opinion, inconsistent with the spirit of a free constitution; for by the nature of a free constitution, the people must consent to laws before they can be obliged in consequence to obey them."

Mobs Opposed to Imperial Law.

The determination of Massachusetts to support her colony-rights against the power of parliament and the prerogative of the king, is evident from the speeches of the leading orators; from the sermons of leading preachers; from pamphlets and newspapers. With these the temper of the people was in harmony, as shown by the mobs which rose against the laws, and the officers, and the property of the British government. Witness the mob that hung up Oliver in effigy; the mob that burned the records of the admiralty court; the mob that attacked the house of Governor Hutchinson, and destroyed his furniture, and scattered his plate and books and papers; the mob that pelted the officers of customs with stones and bricks; the mob that tarred and feathered one who gave information against the breaking of the acts of trade passed by parliament; the mob that rose in opposition to the soldiers; the mob that threw the tea overboard. These mobs were symptomatic of the spirit that pervaded Massachusetts in opposition to parliament and its prerogative, and the defence of colony rights and local laws.

The Supremacy of Local Law Asserted.

Certain violations of the colony rights and local laws are mentioned in the report of a Boston committee, November 22d, 1772, namely, the imposition by parliament of taxes without the consent of the people; the appointment of officers unknown to the charter, supported by the income derived from such taxes; the introduction of fleets and armies to compel obedience to unconstitutional laws; the extension of the powers of the court of admiralty; the act relating to dock-yards and stores, which deprived the people of the right of trial by their peers in the vicinage, and the assumption of absolute legislative powers.

Massachusetts claimed for her people, as men, as colonists, as subjects of the crown, the right to life, liberty, and property; the sole right to manage their internal institutions and concerns; the sole right of raising money from themselves by taxation; the right of being tried by their peers in the vicinage; the right of freely discussing public measures; the right of being governed by the civil as superior to the military power; the right of being free from unreasonable searches, which was violated by the writs of assistance. These and other rights having been violated by the British parliament or British king, Massachusetts was ready to declare herself a free, sovereign, and independent state.

The Supremacy of Local Law Maintained.

For something like a year before July 4th, 1776, Massachusetts, standing on her colony rights, enjoyed a virtual independence. The supremacy of her local laws she was prepared to maintain.

And in April, 1776, the general court passed a resolve to alter the style of writs and other legal processes, substituting the "people and government of Massachusetts" for "George the

Third." Thus Massachusetts, in asserting and maintaining the supremacy of the local law, was the first of the "old thirteen" states independent. Thus was she fully prepared to make a public and formal declaration by her delegates Samuel Adams, John Adams, Robert Treat Paine, Elbridge Gerry, that Massachusetts "was, and of right ought to be, a free and independent state; that she was absolved from all allegiance to the British crown." After a seven years' war in defence of the right to be governed by her own local laws, by treaty with Great Britain she was acknowledged a "free, sovereign, and independent state," in which her own local laws were supreme. Thus Massachusetts having contended strenuously from 1628 until 1776 for colony rights, and local law, was prepared, when she became a sovereign state, having the right to command, to contend strenuously for state rights and local law. Acting in concert with the other states, she, before the world, vindicated the right of the people of Massachusetts to abolish a government when in her opinion, it becomes destructive of the ends for which it was established, and establish such a form of government as she shall judge best.

Massachusetts a Sovereign State.

Massachusetts in 1776, having become a free, sovereign and independent state, proceeded to exercise its sovereignty or right of command. She raised troops; made war; laid taxes; established a mint, and coined money; required the oath of allegiance; enacted laws against treason; punished such as continued loyal to Great Britain. These principles she incorporated in her constitution in 1780, in which she declares herself a sovereign state.

Articles of Confederation.

When the continental congress in November, 1777, "agreed upon a plan of confederacy, securing the freedom, sovereignty, and independence of the (several) United States," and sent it, under the title of "Articles of Confederation," to the several state legislatures, Massachusetts, by the act of her legislature, readily adcpted it. In the second article of that compact are the following words: "Each state retains its sovereignty, freedom and independence." These Massachusetts had contended for successfully, in the halls of legislation, and on the battle field, and these she retained.

In February, 1787, the subject of a convention for revising the articles of confederation being under consideration in the congress, Nathan Dane, of Massachusetts, opposed the movement. "He was at bottom unfriendly to the plan of a convention, and dissuaded his state from going into it." (Eliott's *Debates*, vol. v, 96.)

Convention for Forming a New Federal Constitution.

March 11th, 1787, p. 106, "Massachusetts has also appointed (delegates to the convention). Messrs. Gorham, Dane, King, Gerry, and Strong, compose her deputation." The resolution under which they act, restrains them from acceding to any departure from the principles of the fifth article of confederation. It is conjectured that this fetter, which originated with the senate, will be struck off. Its being introduced at all denotes a very different spirit, in that quarter, from what some had been led to expect." The fifth article, which the legislature of Massachusetts was unwilling to have altered, is as follows:

"For the more convenient management of the general interests of the United States, delegates shall be annually appointed in such manner as the legislature of each state shall direct, to meet in congress on the first Monday in November, in every year, with a power reserved to each state to recall its delegates, or any of them, at any time within the year, and to send others in their stead for the remainder of the year.

"No state shall be represented in congress by less than two, nor by more than seven members; and no person shall be capable of being a delegate for more than three years in any term of six years; nor shall any person, being a delegate, be capable of holding any office under the United States, for which he, or another for his benefit, receives any salary, fees, or emoluments of any kind.

"Each state shall maintain its own delegates in a meeting of the states, and while they act as members of the committee of the states.

"In determining questions in the United States in congress assembled, each state shall have one vote.

"Freedom of speech and debate in congress shall not be impeached or questioned in any court or place out of congress; and the members of congress shall be protected in their persons from arrests and imprisonment, during the time of their going to and from attendance on congress, except for treason, felony or breach of peace."

This article is a very strong assertion of the doctrine of state rights and of the high estimate of the people of Massachusetts of the value of local laws.

The Federal Convention.

The convention for altering the federal constitution, namely the articles of confederation, assembled May 25, 1787, and continued in session until September 17th. On the subject of state rights, the course of Massachusetts in that convention was not as distinct as that of Connecticut in favor, or as that of Virginia in opposition. She acted sometimes with the larger states for the abridgment of those rights, and sometimes with the smaller states for the preservation of those rights. On the great question, whether the states shall have an equal vote in the senate, the vote of Massachusetts was equally divided and thus lost. Mr. Gerry and Mr. Strong voted in the affirmative, Mr. Gorham and Mr. King in the negative. The reason why Mr. Gorham and Mr. King went against state rights was, that they were willing that Massachusetts, Virginia and Pennsylvania, on account of their greater population, should be the leading states. Massachusetts in this way would have the preeminence in New England in the senate, just as she wished to have the preeminence under the federal constitution of 1643.

On the question of giving to the federal government the power to issue paper money and making it a legal tender, Massachusetts was opposed to giving this power and thus enlarging the power of the federal government. On the motion for striking out from the proposed constitution, "and emit bills of credit," Massachusetts with the majority voted in the affirmative, and probably for the same reason that influenced Connecticut and Virginia, as stated by Mr. Madison, namely: to "cut off all pretext for a paper currency, and particularly for making the bills a tender for public or private debts." Massachusetts had seen the evils of continental money, and she was unwilling to repeat those evils. She was prescient of the future, and was unwilling to give any authority to the federal government to issue bills and make them a legal tender.

The State Convention for Adopting the New Federal Constitution.

The state convention of Massachusetts, for adopting the new federal constitution, assembled January 9th, 1788, and continued in session until February 7th, 1788. The constitution encountered great opposition, chiefly on the ground that it was supposed to interfere with state and personal rights. Massachusetts had contended too long and too earnestly for these rights, to give them to the federal government. This opposition would have prevailed, had not certain amendments been proposed, which would if adopted into that instrument, secure their liberties. These amendments proposed by the convention of Massachusetts were nine in number, and as it was confidently expected that they would be adopted by the states, the convention, by the small majority of nineteen, ratified the constitution, one hundred and eighty seven voting for it, and one hundred and sixty-eight against it.

Amendments Proposed by Massachusetts.

First. That it be explicitly declared, that all powers not expressly delegated by the aforesaid constitution, are reserved to the several states, to be by them exercised.

Secondly. That there shall be one representative to every thirty thousand persons, according to the census mentioned in the constitution, until the whole number of representatives amounts to two hundred.

Thirdly. That congress do not exercise the powers vested in them by the 4th section of the 1st article, but in cases where a state shall neglect or refuse to make the regulations therein mentioned, or shall make regulations subversive of the rights of the people to a free and equal representation in congress, agreeably to the constitution.

Fourthly. That congress do not lay direct taxes, but when the moneys arising from the impost and excise are insufficient for the public exigencies, nor then, until congress shall have first made a requisition upon the states, to assess, levy, and pay their respective proportion of such requisitions, agreeably to the census fixed in the said constitution, in such way and manner as the legislatures of the states shall think best; and, in such case, if any state shall neglect or refuse to pay its proportion, pursuant to such requisition, then congress may assess and levy such state's proportion, together with interest thereon, at the rate of six per cent. per annum, from the time of payment prescribed in such requisitions.

Fifthly. That congress erect no company with exclusive advantages of commerce.

Sixthly. That no person shall be tried for crime, by which he may incur an infamous punishment, or loss of life, until he be first indicted by a grand jury, except in such cases as may arise in the government and regulation of the land and naval forces.

Seventhly. The supreme judicial federal court shall have no jurisdiction of causes between citizens of different states, unless the matter in dispute, whether it concern the realty or personalty, be of the value of three thousand dollars at the least; nor shall the federal judicial powers extend to any action between citizens of different states, where the matter in dispute, whether it concern the realty or personalty, is not of the value of fifteen hundred dollars at least.

Eighthly. In civil actions between citizens of different states, every issue of fact arising in actions at common law, shall be tried by a jury, if the parties, or either of them, request it.

Ninthly. Congress shall at no time consent that any person holding an office of trust or profit, under the United States, shall accept of a title of nobility, or any other title or office, from any king, prince, or foreign state.

Character of the Amendments Proposed.

These nine amendments proposed by Massachusetts contain a strong assertion of the doctrine of state rights, intended as they were to limit the powers of the federal government. Read the debates in the Massachusetts convention, read these amendments proposed, and you will be convinced that she was as jealous of any encroachments on state rights as she had ever been of encroachments on colony rights. The end aimed at, in these nine amendments, is declared to be, "*more effectually to guard against an undue administration of the federal government.*" The ratification is called "*an explicit and solemn compact.*" The convention evidently well understood that it was prepared *by* the states; that it was "done in the convention by the unanimous consent of the states present;" that it was formed *for* the states as states; that "the ratification of nine states was sufficient for the constitution *between* the states so ratifying the same;" that it could be amended by the states, and abolished by the states; that the states created the constitution and could destroy it.

The first amendment proposed distinctly shows what was the opinion of the Massachusetts convention on the subject of state rights. *First.* That it be explicitly declared, that all powers not expressly delegated by the aforesaid constitution are reserved to the several states, to be by them exercised. The reserved powers were not to be dormant, but to be asserted and "exercised by the states." It is evident that without the recommendation of these nine amendments, and the expectation that they would substantially be incorporated into the new federal constitution, Massachusetts would have rejected it.

Bradford declares that "the great object of these amendments was to secure the rights of individuals charged on suspicion with treasonable acts against the United States, or with violations of the laws of congress; and to preserve to the respective state governments all the authority and power not clearly vested in the general government by the *federal compact.*"

Legislation after the Adoption of the Federal Constitution.

The Massachusetts convention adopted the federal constitution February 7th, 1788. The legislature of Massachusetts, in aid of that provision of the constitution intended to secure the restoration of fugitive slaves to their masters, passed a law by which negroes were prohibited, under the penalty of confinement, hard labor in the house of correction, and whipping not exceeding ten stripes, from taking up their residence in the state.

Thus Massachusetts asserted her own state rights, and recognized the rights of the slave holding states, and her own obligations to deliver up fugitive slaves to their masters.

The Position of Massachusetts in the Federal Union.

From the foregoing statements, we can understand the historical position of Massachusetts in the federal union.

In the year 1787, Massachusetts as a "free, sovereign and independent state," sent delegates to the federal convention which framed the federal constitution, by which the present union of the American states was subsequently consummated. In this convention the voting was *by states*, and not by the numerical majority of the delegates.

In the year 1788, Massachusetts, acting for herself and by herself, and binding herself, and not Rhode Island, adopted the federal constitution. Massachusetts bound herself, and not Rhode Island, as this latter state did not accede to the union until 1790, when she, as a sovereign state, bound herself by her own act, as a party to the compact.

Thus Massachusetts became, in the language of Washington, "a member of the union," one of the states united by the new federal constitution. Thus the states, as states, formed the union, and not the people of America as a mass. The union is a union of states, and not a union of the mass of the people of the several states. Massachusetts — a "nation," in the language of Montesquieu, who spoke of the colonies as "becoming so many great nations;" Kent, vol. i, p. 274; a "republic," in the language of Lord Clarendon, who spoke of the colonies as "hardened into republics" — entered into a compact with the other nations, twelve of them, into a compact with the other republics, twelve of them, to form, so far as foreign nations were concerned, one nation. Thus, externally, the United States of America became, in the language of Kossuth, a "republic composed of republics."

That New Hampshire, Massachusetts, Rhode Island, Connecticut, and the other states of the old thirteen, by entering into the constitutional compact, formed a *confederated* and not a consolidated republic, there is evidence that cannot be gainsaid. In the first congress which assembled under the present federal constitution, President Washington having been inaugurated, the senate made an address to him in which they say:

"We beg you to be assured that the senate will at all times cheerfully cooperate in any measure that may strengthen the union and conduce to the happiness and perpetuate the liberties of this great *confederated* republic." (See vol. I, Benton's *Debates*, p. 13).

The president (Washington) in reply says: "I am happy to learn that the senate will at all times cooperate in every measure which may tend to promote the welfare of this *confederated* republic." Vol. I, Benton, p. 15.

In 1836, John Quincy Adams, of Massachusetts, in the debate in congress on the admission of Arkansas as a state (see 13 Benton's *Debates*, p. 33), speaks of congress as the "representative of that *federation* compounded partly of slaveholding, and partly of entirely free states."

Contemporary Opinion of Massachusetts Statesmen.

Theophilus Parsons, in the convention of Massachusetts that adopted the present federal constitution, remarks: "Congress has only a concurrent right with each state in levying direct taxes, not an exclusive right; and the right of each state to direct taxation is equally *extensive and perfect as the right of congress;* any law, therefore, of the United States for securing to congress *more than concurrent right with each state is usurpation and is void.*" What would he have said to the usurpations which have since been committed by the federal government?

In another speech in the same convention, Chief Justice Parsons said: "An act of usurpation [by the federal government] is not obligatory, it is not law; and any man is justified in his resistance. Let him be considered as a criminal by the general government, yet only his fellow-citizens can convict him; they are his jury, and if they pronounce him innocent, not all the powers of congress can hurt him; and innocent they certainly will pronounce him, if the supposed law he resisted was an act of usurpation."

Samuel Adams, always distinguished for his devotedness to colony rights and state rights, said of the first proposed amendment to the constitution already quoted, in favor of it, that it was "consonant with the second article in the present confederation that each state retains its sovereignty, freedom, and independence, and that every power, jurisdiction, and right which is not by this confederation expressly delegated to the United States in congress assembled." When appointed lieutenant governor of Massachusetts, John Hancock being governor, he said: "I shall be called upon to make a declaration, and I shall do it cheerfully, that the commonwealth of Massachusetts is, and of right ought to be, a free, sovereign, and independent state. I shall be called upon to make another declaration with the same solemnity *to support the constitution of the United States.* I see no inconsistency in this, for it must be intended that these constitutions should mutually aid and support each other."

James Sullivan, in 1791, speaking of the federal constitution says: "Here they represent the really one *separate and sovereign power*, forming no civil relation to each other than what might result from a voluntary and uncompulsory *compact.*" Here this very eminent man, attorney general of the state, and afterward judge of the supreme court, and governor of the state, speaks of the federal constitution as "a *compact* between the states." He also adds: "Nevertheless, if each state does not retain its sovereignty in some things, there is no union of several existings tates but an entire government." So again he says, p. 28: "Treason is a violation of the duties of allegiance to an established government, holding the exercise of sovereign power; and there can be no such crime unless committed against such authority." But the federal constitution recognizes treason *against a state*, and thus recognizes the sovereignty of the several states.

Bradford, in his *History*, p. 12, remarks that there might have been two-thirds of the states in favor of the constitution, without there being two-thirds of the whole population of all the states." And again, "the federal features prevail and give the character to the *compact.*"

Thus Massachusetts understood that the constitution was a *compact* between the states, just as Gouverneur Morris, who wrote it, understood it; that this compact formed a *confederacy* of states, just as Judge Marshall understood it, and that each state is sovereign and entitled to the allegiance of its citizens. Thus Judge Marshall in his *Life of Washington*, vol. v., page 133, says: "North Carolina and Rhode Island did not at first accept of the constitution, and New York was dragged into it by a repugnance to being excluded from the *confederacy.*"

SUABILITY OF STATES.

In 1793, the governor (John Hancock), and the attorney-general (James Sullivan), were summoned by the United States marshal to appear in court and answer to a suit of an individual belonging to another state. This summons the governor refused to obey. He then summoned a meeting of the legislature. In his opening speech he said: " I cannot conceive that the people of this commonwealth, who, by their representatives in convention adopted the *federal compact*, expected a state would be held liable to answer a compulsory civil process to an individual of another state or a foreign kingdom." And in the same speech he expressed an opinion in favor of state rights and of the sovereignty of the states in all cases not expressly or plainly prohibited by the federal constitution. He also said that a " consolidation of the states into one government would endanger the nation as a republic, and eventually *divide the states now united, or eradicate* the principles for which we have contended." These " principles " were the principles of the revolution. In view of these facts, the legislature, on the twenty-seventh of September, 1793, passed the following: " *Resolved*, That a power claimed of compelling the state to become a defendant in the court of the United States, at the suit of an individual or individuals, is unnecessary and inexpedient, and in its exercise dangerous to the power, safety, and independence of the several states, and *repugnant to the first principles of a confederate government.*"

Accordingly, the legislature of Massachusetts proposed the amendment to the federal constitution, which was adopted, and is known as the eleventh article of the amendments. Besides John Hancock and James Sullivan, other leading men took an active part in favor of state rights and the amendment to the constitution. Among them should be mentioned Samuel Adams, Dr. Jarvis, and Nathan Dane. Samuel Adams was always a consistent advocate or defender of state rights, just as he had been of colony rights. He had taken the leading part, unless Otis or Hancock was entitled to that honor, in obtaining the independence of Massachusetts, and he wished to preserve that independence under the new confederation formed by the new federal constitution.

7

A Parallel between Colony Rights and State Rights.

These two classes of rights, existing at different periods, are equivalents of each other. Colony rights, under the British government, bore the same relation to charters conferred by the king, which state rights under the federal government bear to the federal constitution. The colonists of Massachusetts, from 1620 to 1776, contended earnestly for their colony rights. The citizens of Massachusetts, from 1776 to the present time, have contended earnestly for state rights. The reasons in each case were substantially the same. These reasons lie in the great fact that the liberties of each individual depended on maintaining colony rights in the one case and state rights in the other. Accordingly, the friends of liberty have been the friends, and the enemies of liberty have been the enemies, of colony rights and of state rights.

It should, however, be borne in mind that colony rights were "granted" rights — that is, rights granted by the king, in the specific charter, or by former kings as in *Magna Charta* and embodied in the British constitution. But state rights are *reserved* rights — that is, rights reserved by the states, when they delegated several powers to the federal government. The colonies, therefore, had to take upon themselves the burden of showing or proving what rights were granted to them in the charter under which they severally acted, or by the British constitution. If the British government encroached upon the granted rights, it was guilty of tyranny which ought to be resisted. But the states are obliged to take upon themselves no such burden, for it rests upon the federal government to prove what powers are delegated to it, and if it goes beyond the delegated powers and encroaches upon the reserved powers, it is guilty of tyranny which ought to be resisted.

It is a little remarkable that the advocates of colony rights in Massachusetts regarded the charter as a solemn compact between the king and the colony, binding both parties, while the British government and the advocates of the royal prerogative regarded it like the charter of a petty corporation in England, repealable at pleasure, or to be disregarded when the necessities or the convenience of the crown should require it to be disregarded. In like manner the advocates of state rights in Massachusetts have regarded the federal constitution as a solemn compact between the states, binding the parties, namely, the states, and limiting the federal government to *the use only of delegated powers ;* while the opposers of state rights attribute to the federal government such large undefined powers under the federal constitution as to deprive the states of their sovereignty, and reduce them very much to the condition of petty corporations. Thus the federal government, according to this last view of it, is the political equivalent, in the present system, of the British government in the colonial system, but with larger powers and a more despotic use of them.

The Purchase of Louisiana.

The purchase of Louisiana took place in 1803, its admission into the federal union in 1812. The statesmen and people of Massachusetts justly regarded this measure, by which the relative importance of the state of Massachusetts would be abridged, as not sanctioned by the constitution, and therefore exonerating the state from its *obligation to remain in the federal union thus violated and broken.*

So thoroughly convinced was Alexander Hamilton that there was a plan in progress for the separation of the union, that on June 11th, 1804, on the Saturday previous to his death, he said to Col. John Trumbull, "with a look of deep meaning," "You are going to Boston. You will see the principal men there. Tell them from *me*, as *my* request, for God's sake to cease their conversation and threatenings about the separation of the union. It must hang together as long as it can be made to." (Hamilton's *History of the Republic*, vol. VII, p. 822.)

The Embargo.

The embargo was laid by congress on the 22d of December, 1807. In 1808, there were strong demonstrations of opposition to it. We have the authority of John Quincy Adams for saying that "the people were constantly instigated to forcible resistance against it, and juries often acquitted the violators of it upon the ground that it was unconstitutional, assumed in the face of a solemn decision of the district court of the United States." A separation of the union was stimulated in the public prints, and a convention of delegates from the New England states to meet in New Haven, was intended and proposed.

Mr. John Quincy Adams, in his letter to Mr. Giles, urged that "a continuance of the embargo much longer would certainly be met by forcible resistance, supported by the legislature [of Massachusetts], and probably by the judiciary of the state.". . . . "That the object of the leaders had been, for several years, the *dissolution of the union*, and the establishment of a separate confederation, he knew from unequivocal evidence, although not provable in a court of law." Niles's *Register*, vol. xxxv., p. 138. In consequence of this opposition to it the embargo was repealed, March 1st, 1809, just before the retirement of Mr. Jefferson from the presidential office.

The War of 1812.

On the 18th day of June, 1812, war was declared by the United States against Great Britain. When, soon after, a requisition was made upon Massachusetts for forty-one companies of artillery and infantry, Governor Caleb Strong refused compliance with the order issued by General Dearborn, notwithstanding the secretary of war wrote to him urging his compliance. In a message to the legislature, in allusion to this refusal to furnish troops to the general government, he said, "I was fully disposed to comply with the requirements of the constitution of the United States, and the laws made in pursuance thereof, and sincerely regret that a request should be made by an officer of the national government with which I could not constitutionally comply. But it appeared to me that the requisition was of this character, and I was under the *same obligation to maintain the rights of the states*, as to support the constitution of the United States." The course pursued by the governor was in accordance with the declared opinion of the judges of the supreme court on the constitutionality of the requisition, aad was approved by the legislature and the people of Massachusetts (See *Massachusetts Reports*, vol. viii., p. 548).

The Hartford Convention.

In consequence of applications from many of the towns, the legislature of Massachusetts appointed delegates to a convention in Hartford, held December 15th, 1814. This convention, having its origin in Massachusetts, was attended by delegates from that state, Connecticut, Rhode Island, New Hampshire, and Vermont, who were twenty-six in number. For intelligence and moral worth, for patriotism and dignified deportment, they would compare favorably with any body of men that ever assembled in this country.

After a session of three weeks they made a report, which was approved by the legislature of Massachusetts by a strong vote. The committee of the legislature, in their report on the doings of the convention, say: "The committee entertain a high sense of the wisdom and ability with which this convention have discharged their arduous trust; and while they maintain the principle of state sovereignty, and of the duties which citizens owe to their respective state governments, they give the most satisfactory proofs of attachment to the constitution of the United States and to the national union." This report was adopted by the house, by a vote of one hundred and fifty-nine to forty-eight. "The governor was empowered to appoint three commissioners to proceed immediately to the seat of the national government, requesting the consent of the federal congress to the measures recommended by the convention." The commissioners thus appointed were Thomas H. Perkins, Harrison Gray Otis, and William Sullivan.

Of the seven amendments to the constitution proposed by the convention, and approved by the legislature of Massachusetts, all but one, or possibly two, are intended to limit the power of the federal government, and thus to increase the power of the several states. (See Dwight's *History of the Hartford Convention*).

Opinions of the Nature of the Federal Union.

It should be borne in mind that Governor Strong was one of the delegates to the convention in Philadelphia, which framed the constitution, and could hardly have failed to understand what were the provisions of that instrument. It is believed that every member of the Hartford convention was born before the declaration of independence, that several were personally active in procuring the adoption of the federal constitution, and that all were devotedly attached to the union, created by that compact.

A careful study of the history of Massachusetts for above

thirty years from the adoption of the federal constitution, will show that her leading men, generally, were as devotedly attached to the rights reserved to the states as they were to the powers delegated to the federal government. They regarded the state as competent to take care of its *internal* institutions, and they regarded any encroachment upon *the right of the state to manage its internal concerns as a usurpation.* They had asserted that right from the first settlement of the commonwealth, under the constitution of 1643, under the old confederation, and under the new confederation, formed by the present federal constitution.

"The *allegiance* they owe to this commonwealth as a sovereign independent state." (*Answer of the house of representatives to the governor*, October, 1810).

"This commonwealth forms an important member of the national *confederacy.*" (*Answer of the house to the governor*, 1810).

"If an extensive confederate republic is to be maintained, and we fervently pray that it may, it can only be by a free communication of the grievances felt, and the evils apprehended by any of the members, and by prompt and liberal remedies." (*Remonstrance by the legislature of Massachusetts to the hon. senate and house of reperesentatives in congress assembled*, June 14, 1813).

February, 1814, the legislature passed an act by which no prisoners of war were allowed to be placed in the jails of Massachusetts except by *judicial* authority, and all prisoners of war were required to be discharged from said jails in thirty days, unless sooner discharged by the authority of the United States.

On the right inherent in the individual of discussing public measures, and the duty of the state to protect each individual thus doing, the senate in answer to the governor, 1814, made the following declaration: "And may it please your excellency, in the apprehension of this senate, this duty is as incumbent and imperious in a state of war as in a state of peace; union among the people is essential to the success of the government, being necessarily subordinate to the *fundamental doctrine* that in every state of things, in a free country, the right of discussing public measures is essential to the liberties of the people."

Resolve on the Admission of Texas.

The following resolve was passed by the Massachusetts legislature in 1845.

"*Resolved*, That Massachusetts hereby refuses to acknowledge the act of the government of the United States, authorizing the admission of Texas, as a legal act in any way binding her from using her utmost exertions, in cooperation with her sister states, by every lawful and constitutional measure, to annul its condition, and defeat its accomplishment."

In this as in other cases, Massachusetts claims the right to judge concerning the legality and the constitutionality of the acts of the Federal government, and to adopt such measures as she judges constitutional to defeat those acts.

Daniel Webster's Matured Opinions.

From the time that he delivered his speech on the seventh of March, 1850, to the day of his lamented death, all of his speeches, that have come under the writer's notice, recognize the doctrine of state rights, especially of the right of each state to manage *its own internal concerns*. In his speech delivered at the dinner given him by the *Reform convention of Maryland*, at Annapolis, March 25, 1851, Mr. Webster used the following language:

"In the lapse of years, and in the rising of one generation after another, it may very possibly happen, and we are sure that it does happen, and has happened, that the exact principles of the union of these states are not always properly understood. It may not be amiss to recur, now, to what I conceive to be the *original principle* upon which these colonies were united, the objects for which they were united, and the limitation to these objects. These thirteen colonies, all of English origin, were settled on this continent at different times and under different circumstances. They had differences of local laws and administrations; they wére, some of them, quite remote from one another; but they were all subject to the crown of England.

"And when, in the course of events, they all thought, and thought truly, they had just cause of complaint against the tyranny of England, their object was to unite in a common cause against a common enemy. How unite? For what purposes unite? For what ends unite? Why it never entered into their conceptions that they were to consolidate themselves into one integral government; that they were to cease to be Virgina, Maryland, Massachusetts, and Carolina. Not at all. But they were to unite for those great purposes which should enable them to make a stand against the English government. They were to unite for the common defence and the general welfare. They were to come to an agreement upon things necessary to that purpose, and nothing else."

"When all the colonies came together for the general purpose of defencc against a common enemy, what did they do? Did they seek to merge and confound and consolidate all these states into one great community? No such thing. They meant to unite upon those objects which were necessary for the common defence; and they meant to have every thing else in the control of the states, to do just as they thought proper. That was a day of liberality and justice. It was a day in which religious opinions produced no effect upon the general sentiments of the country, in regard to the associations of the states for common objects. Why sir, did any body at the North; did any protestant, descending from ancestors in limiting the principles of CROMWELL or of HENRY VANE, whoever he was, feel any less confidence in the integrity and entire patriotism of CHARLES CARROLL, because he was a catholic? Not at all. Nor did Maryland hesitate to accord the meed of patriotism, whenever it was due, to the ADAMSES, to ALEXANDER HAMILTON, to RUFUS KING, or whoever else belonged to the North, because they were of different sentiments in religion. Their association was political. It was founded on general policy and union; a sort of confederacy, at that time, to resist the common enemy, and to do what was necessary for the common good. Gentlemen, I hope for one, *never to see this original idea departed from.*"

PERSONAL LIBERTY BILL PASSED MAY 21, 1855.

Section 10th.

"Any person who shall grant any certificate, under or by virtue of the acts of congress, mentioned in the 9th sec. (Acts of 1793, and 1850), shall be deemed to have resigned any commission from the commonwealth, that he may possess, and his office shall be deemed vacant; and he shall forever thereafter be inelegible to any office of trust, honor, or emolument, under the laws of this commonwealth.

Section 11th.

Any person who shall act as counsel, or attorney, for any claimant, of any alleged fugitive from service or labor, under, or by virtue of the acts of congress mentioned in the 9th section of this act, shall be deemed to have resigned any commission from the commonwealth, that he may possess, and he shall be, thereafter, incapacitated from appearing as counsel or attorney, in the courts of the commonwealth."

These are portions of the Personal Liberty bill, intended to nullify acts of congress passed in 1793, and in 1850, and also that article in the constitution, which relates to fugitive slaves.

In 1857, Edward G. Loring, a United States commissioner, under the fugitive slave bill, passed by congress in 1850, was by the legislature, turned out of the office of judge of probate, because he did not obey this unconstitutional Liberty bill. What makes his removal the more remarkable was, that he was appointed to the office of judge, while he was already a commissioner.

The principal charge against him in the address reported, was, "That he consented to sit as a United States slave commissioner, in defiance of the moral sentiment of Massachusetts, as expressed by the legislature of 1850."

Judge Loring was required to regard the laws of Massachusetts as paramount to the laws of congress.

Governor Boutwell, in the following extract from his message in 1851 very properly describes the provision of the constitution for the delivery of fugitives as in the nature of a treaty. This description can be extended to apply to the whole constitution, as a compact between the sovereign states as parties. Massachusetts, by her personal liberty bills, furnished the fullest evidence that she was willing to break that article of the treaty. She did practically and persistently break that article of the treaty, and thus released the states injured by her acts from their obligations to her under the same treaty. The doctrine prevalent in Massachusetts was enunciated in the following declaration brought before the senate, in resolves: "We hold it to be the duty of that body (congress) to pass such laws only in regard thereto (the return of fugitive slaves) as will be sustained by the public sentiment of the free states where such laws are to be enforced." According to this view, "the public sentiment of the free states" should form the measure of congressional enactment in respect to the interests of slaveholding states.

Governor Briggs.

Extract from a report of a committee to the legislature of Massachusetts on the proposed repeal of the personal liberty bill, April 11th, 1856, of which Governor Briggs, then a member of the house, was chairman:

"With his excellency (Governor Gardner) we believe that of the state rights retained by each sovereign member of the confederacy, the two cardinal ones are the *habeas corpus* and *the trial by jury.*

"It was not that the states *relinquished* these rights to the keeping and protection of the federal government; but so unquestionable and paramount to the sovereignty of every human institution were they esteemed, that they (the states) took care to provide against the remote and improbable contingency of any state so far departing from the faith of the fathers, as to be consenting to yield or compromise these great principles. It was a mutual agreement among the states, to prevent any state so disposed, from abrogating the cardinal principles of a free government to deprive the citizens of these rights. It was a power conferred to preserve and protect, not to attack and destroy. The bill of rights and constitution of the states, old and new, attests they never parted with *their fundamental principles of sovereignty*, the indispensable condition of the very existence of a free government, the right and duty to protect the rights and liberties of its citizens and subjects.

"State sovereignty, on all subjects and in all things when the exercise of that sovereignty has not been delegated to the United States, is the language of the constitution and the safety of the states. This principle has *always* been regarded as vital to the existence and perpetuity of the states, a distinct and independent power. It was so claimed by the fathers and founders of our institutions. It is as earnestly cherished by their posterity, the true patriots and statesmen of the present generation." The committee, on the ground of state rights, was opposed to the repeal of the personal liberty bill, though declared to be unconstitutional by the highest judicial authority in the state.

Case of Senator Sumner.

Resolve passed by the legislature of Massachusetts, May, 1856:

"*Resolved*, That the legislature of Massachusetts is imperatively called upon by the plainest dictates of duty, from a decent regard to the rights of her citizens, and a respect for her character as a soverign state, to demand, and the legislature hereby does demand of the national congress a prompt and strict investigation into the recent assault upon Senator Sumner, and the expulsion by the house of Mr. Brooks, of South Carolina, and every other member concerned with him in said assault."

Here Massachusetts, the constituent of the federal government, demands of her agent, viz. the federal congress to whom she delegated certain powers when she adopted the constitution in 1788, the performance of a certain duty which she assigned to that agent.

The Dred Scott Decision.

Resolve in relation to the decision of the supreme court of the United States, in the case of Dred Scott versus Sanford, March 27, 1858:

"*Resolved*, That all citizens of Massachusetts are citizens of the United States; that all negroes not aliens, domiciled within her limits, are citizens of Massachusetts and are entitled to all the rights, privileges and immunities of citizenship in the courts of the United states."

Kansas.

In 1855, the legislature passed resolutions, one of which was "that this commonwealth is ready, if necessary, to aid with her whole power, the governor of Kansas and the people of that territory, or of any other territory or state in support of constitutional rights by whomsoever infringed;" the commonwealth being the judge as to what rights are constitutional.

March 31, 1857, Mr. Wells, a leading member of the legislature, and acting with a majority of the house, in a speech on the Kansas resolution says:

"The sovereignty of Massachusetts is older than that of the union, and was not conferred by the union. The declaration of independence is an avowal of state rights. The treaty of peace, 1783, released to each state its sovereignty and freedom. The right of allegiance was transferred, not to the United States, but to each state. The articles of confederation declared that each state should retain its sovereignty, freedom and independence. The powers of the United States are all *granted* by the several states."

Mr. Upham, in the senate, May 7, 1857:

"The American union, as a body politic, consists exclusively of states, separate, and states confederated. Whatever does not belong to a state, as one of the constituent parts of the system, is not properly embraced by, or in accordance with the true theory of our government."

Rufus Choate on the Preservation of the Union.

"I have sometimes thought that the states in our system, may be compared to the primordial particles of matter, indivisible, indestructible, impenetrable, whose natural condition is to repel each other, or at best, to exist in their own independent identity while the Union is an artificial aggregation of such particles.

"Have you ever considered that it was a federative system we had to adopt, and that in such a system a conflict of head and members is in some form, and to some extent, a result of course? There the states were when we became a nation. There they had been for one hundred and fifty years, for one hundred and seventy years. * * In the scheme of every statesman they remained a component part unannihilated, indestructible. In the scheme of the constitution, of compromise itself they remained a component part, indestructible. In the theories of all publicists and all speculators, they were retained, and they were valued for it to hinder and disarm that centralization which had been found to be the danger and the weakness of federal liberty." (*Rufus Choate's Address on the Fourth of July*, 1858).

The relation between the state, and the United States, as a federal relation, and *only* a federal relation.

In the language of Governor Banks, in his speech to the legislature, 1866: "She (Massachusetts) recognizes the existence of state and national governments, each sovereign and independent in its own sphere of action, and dividing the jurisdiction between them, not by territorial limits, and not by the relation of superior and subordinate, but classifying the subjects of government, and designating those over which each has entire and independent control."

The states sustain to each other international relations, as declared by the supreme court of the United States.

From the facts stated above it is manifest:

I. That Massachusetts has regarded herself, at least since the revolution and treaty of peace with Great Britain, as a sovereign state; as a free state; as an independent state.

II. That in 1788, Massachusetts formed a union with the other states, namely, a confederated or a federal union, or a confederacy, in which each state preserves its individuality and government.

III. That this federal or confederated union was formed by a compact "between the states," to which each state is a party.

IV. That this compact between the states is a constitution; just as the agreement between individuals on board the May Flower, is, in the language of Bancroft, a compact, and in the language of Mr. Webster, a constitution; just as the state constitution formed by individuals in Massachusetts is declared in that instrument to be a *compact* just as the articles of the old confederation is declared by George T. Curtis to be a compact between the states, and by General Washington to be a constitution.

V. That as a party to the constitutional compact by which the federal government was formed, Massachusetts claims the right to judge of the acts of that government, which she helped to create, and which with the other states, she has a right to alter or abolish by altering or abolishing the constitution.

VI. That when any of her citizens, are injured or oppressed by any usurpation of the federal government, Massachusetts is bound to interpose for their protection and relief, she being one of the high contracting parties by which the federal agency was established, and therefore, as a constituent, having a right to call her agent to an account for the use made of "delegated power."

VII. That the same rights for which she contended against the mother country, she is ready, if need be, to contend for against the federal government, as the right to the writ of *habeas corpus*; the right of trial by jury from the vicinage; the right to manage his *internal* concerns; the right of *freedom of speech*, and of the *liberty of the press*; the right of having the *civil* superior to the military authority.

VIII. That the union or confederacy can be preserved only by a free communication of grievances, by any of the suffering members, and a prompt attention on the part of the federal government to those grievances.

IX. That Massachusetts, possessing original sovereignty and having delegated to the federal government the *power to exercise sovereignty* over certain subjects, can resume that power when she finds that it has been abused to her injury and oppression, on the same principles upon which she separated from the mother country as announced in the declaration of independence.

X. That colony rights and state rights are substantially the same, and that the latter require to be cherished and protected as carefully as the former.

XI. That Massachusetts, as possessing original and inherent sovereignty, claims the *allegiance* of all her citizens, while by adopting the federal constitution she has made it obligatory on them to "support the constitution of the United States."

XII. That Massachusetts is authorized both by her own constitution and by the constitution of the United States to punish *treason* as a crime committed against her sovereignty.

XIII. That Massachusetts, at one time or another, has claimed and exercised the right to nullify a law of the United States, when, in her judgment, it is contrary to the federal constitution or to the *higher law* of her own conscience.

Extracts from the State Constitution.

"The people of this commonwealth have the sole and exclusive right of governing themselves as a free, sovereign and independent state; and do, and forever hereafter shall exercise and enjoy every power, jurisdiction and right which is not or may not hereafter be by them expressly delegated to the United States in congress assembled.

"Oath of office. "I, A B, solemnly swear that I will bear true and faithful allegiance to the commonwealth of Massachusetts, and will support the constitution thereof; and that I will faithfully and impartially perform all the duties incumbent on me according to the best of my abilities and understanding agreeably to the constitution and laws of the commonwealth. So help me God."

What are state rights? What is a state? 1. "A state, in the most enlarged sense, means the people composing a particular nation or community. In this sense, the state means the whole people united in one body politic, and the state and the people of a state are equivalent expressions." Judge Wilson in his law lectures, says: "In free states, the people form an artificial person or body politic, the highest that can be known." Each of the United States thus existing became sovereign at the revolution, and by the treaty of peace with Great Britain. In this sense the state of Massachusetts, that is the people of Massachusetts, adopted her own constitution, and the federal constitution. 2. A state means the legislature which means the people, as when we say the state of Massachusetts passed the Maine liquor law. 3. A state means the territory included in physical boundaries. State rights of Massachusetts under the federal constitution, then, are all the rights and powers of a sovereign, free and independent republic or nation, excepting those which she has distinctly and clearly delegated to the federal government.

Dr. Noah Webster, when a citizen of Massachusetts, in his oration before the Washington Benevolent Society, has the following passage: "How can the states, *the parties to the federal compact*, understanding its conditions, and bound in duty to guard their rights, answer to the people and posterity for suffering such a palpable act of arbitrary power [the embargo] to pass into a precedent?" This statement is in harmony with his definition of the word *compact* and his other definitions in his large dictionary.

Dr. Timothy Dwight, a native of Massachusetts, and representative in the general court and afterwards president of Yale College, in writing from Greenfield Hill, 1793, says: "A war with Great Britain, we in New England will not enter into. Sooner would ninety-nine in a hundred of our inhabitants separate from the union than plunge themselves into such an abyss of misery."

"*Would a division of the union be beneficial?*" was one of the mooted questions in Yale College under President Dwight. On this question, Dr. Dwight in one of his decisions says: "By fostering jealousies, creating local feeling in opposition to each other, and indulging violent denunciations, the union of the states may, perhaps, be dissolved; but it will not be suddenly effected. It will be the result of deliberation. Our New Englanders are deliberate in determining, but when they once begin to act they are resolute. If they ever divide the union, it will be because they are forced to do it; and they will not leave their work unfinished." He was opposed to disunion, but does not question the right of secession.

The several Spheres of Local Law.

I. The local law of the homestead, founded on the relations of parent and child, and sanctioned by the word of God. It has been through many generations the law of kindness on the lips and in the life of the parents, calling into exercise all the sweet charities of the family circle.

II. The local law of the school district.

III. The local law of the church. According to which in its early history it established its own covenant, its own confession of faith, its own discipline, its own rules of holy living.

IV. The laws of the town as distinguished from the laws of the colony or state.

V. The laws of the colony as distinguished from the laws of Great Britain.

VI. The laws of the state as distinguished from those of the United States.

What a noble model in these several circles of power, Massachusetts has furnished to the world! The men of Massachusetts in all the generations would permit no encroachments on these laws by others outside of themselves. What Goldsmith said in complimentary terms of his countrymen, can be said of the men of Massachusetts of past generations:—

> Pride in their port, defiance in their eye,
> I see the lords of human kind pass by;
> Fierce in their native hardiness of soul,
> True to imagined right, above control.

The love of local law has been in vigorous exercise ever since the settlement of the two colonies, during the sixty-three years of the continuance of the first charter of Massachusetts; in the reigns of James I, Charles I, Oliver Cromwell, Charles II, and James II. It showed increasing power under the provincial charter, in the reigns of William and Mary, Queen Anne, George I, George II, and George III, when it produced the American revolution. The same love of local law was shown by Massachusetts, as a member of the New England confederacy formed in 1643, as a member of the old confederation formed in the revolutionary war, and as a member of the new or present confederation formed in 1788. It has grown with the growth, and strengthened with the strength of the colony and state. Massachusetts would bear no foreign interference with her local laws.

That they were all judicious and proper in aim and spirit, the most dutiful and affectionate of her sons would not pretend. Society is made up of individuals, and therefore is liable to the same errors to which individuals are subject.

In this inherited love of local law, continued through so many generations, may be seen the personal identity of Massachusetts, through the long period of her existence, as distinctly as the personal identity of an individual who has lived through a long life. In this respect we may say of her, *semper eadem.*

In her whole history, wherever the minions of power went on her soil, they found that the spirit of independence was the *genius loci.*

That spirit is symbolized in the crest and motto of her armorial bearings. On the seal, which represents her personality, the naked sword uplifted in the right hand, is a threat to tyrants. That hand seeks calm quiet with the sword, but it is a quiet under liberty.[1]

[1] The crest and the motto are each incomplete without the other. The motto is the fragment of a sentence composed by the stern opposer of tyranny, Algernon Sidney, in reference to himself. The following is the whole sentence, said to have been written by him in an album.

"*Manus hæc inimica tyrannis*
Ense petit placidam sub libertate quietem."

The crest replaces the first line, and makes the meaning complete and more vivid.

LOCAL LAW IN CONNECTICUT.[1]

Local law is a relative term. It stands contrasted with imperial law. As used in this paper, it means the laws of the town as distinguished from the laws of the colony or the state; moreover it means the laws of the colony or state as distinguished from the laws of Great Britain; or of the United States.

The Towns on the Sea-Side.

In the month of June, 1637, a company of English emigrants arrived in Massachusetts, under the leadership of John Davenport and Theophilus Eaton. Strong inducements were offered them to settle in that colony, near Boston; namely, lands for their habitations, and a place in the civil government for Mr. Eaton, and a place in the synod, to be held that year, for Mr. Davenport.

But they had just escaped from laws made for an empire and not adapted to their local wants, laws made by others and not by themselves. They did not feel inclined to submit themselves to Massachusetts rule, or to involve themselves in the religious disputes then rife there. They had certain ideas of their own, on civil polity and religion, which they wished to carry out; and accordingly after a reconnoissance by some of their number, they came to *Quinnipiac*, now New Haven, in the month of April, 1638, to be subject only to the local laws which they themselves should enact. They had, when in England, suffered enough from ecclesiastical and civil laws made by others; and they determined to make their own local laws and thus enjoy civil and

[1] Read before the New England Historic Genealogical Society, and before the New Haven Colony Historical Society, prepared from the *New England Historical and Genealogical Register* for Jan., 1870.

religious liberty. If, when in England, some of their number enjoyed the right of suffrage in the election of members of the House of Commons, this right was of little practical value, inasmuch as they were overborne by majorities in that branch, or at least by the superincumbent weight of the other two branches of the government.

Soon after their arrival here, they united in a "plantation covenant," in which they declare, "that as in matters that concern the gathering of a church, so likewise in all public offices which concern civil order, as choice of magistrates and officers, making and repealing laws, dividing allotments of inheritance, and all things of a like nature, we would all of us be ordered by the rules which the scripture holds forth to us." This "plantation covenant" was an equivalent of the covenant entered into by the children of Israel, when they went into the promised land; an equivalent of the compact made on board the Mayflower by the settlers of Plymouth. This plantation covenant virtually announces the purpose to make their own local laws, in ecclesiastical and civil concerns, under the teaching of the scriptures interpreted by themselves.

On the 9th of June, 1639, the planters laid the foundation of their ecclesiastical and civil polities. They decided that none but church members should exercise the right of suffrage and provided for the election of seven of their number to be *pillars* of the church to be formed, who should have power to admit others to membership, in accordance with the local law.

The members of the church thus formed being free planters, having the right of suffrage, all met together as one body, on the 25th of October, and took all the civil power into their own hands. This plantation or town meeting they styled the GENERAL COURT. Having adopted the "Freeman's charge" they proceeded to elect a magistrate, namely: THEOPHILUS EATON, and four deputies, namely: ROBERT NEWMAN, MATHEW GILBERT, NATHANIEL TURNER, and THOMAS FUGIL, to assist the magistrates. They also elected Thomas Fugil notary to keep a record of the doings of the general court, and of the doings of the magistrates; and ROBERT SEELY, a marshal to act under the direction of the magistrates.

Thus was the town organized by local law, independent of all other towns. Thus was the church constituted by local law, independent of all other churches. Thus the civil government was formed by local law, independent of all other governments. Thus the body politic, complete in itself, *teres atque rotundus*, acknowledging no earthly superior and no political ally, claimed and exercised the rights of sovereignty and of self-government in the limits of the plantation or town.

The settlers of *Wepauwaug*, or Milford, adopted substantially the same course. They too had their Aaron and Moses: PETER PRUDDEN and WILLIAM FOWLER; their seven "pillars," their independent church, and their independent body politic; their general court, and their magistratical court. There was, however, this difference, that they admitted into their body politic six planters, who were not members of the church.

The settlers of *Menunkatuck*, Guilford, in like manner, had their Aaron and Moses: HENRY WHITFIELD and SAMUEL DESBOROUGH; their seven "*pillars*, their independent church, their independent body politic, their general court, and their magistratical court.

Thus each of these three towns on the sea-side was, in 1639, a separate and independent commonwealth, in which "sovereign law, thė state's collected will, sat empress." In form, in spirit, and affection for each other, they were sisters. In the eyes of their admirers, they stood, each complete in herself; like the three sister Graces on the shore of the Ægean sea, with arms linked in mutual love, each moving at "her own sweet will."

How it was, historically, that these three several communities were formed; what were the elective affinities which held each community together; how it was in each case that the church crystallized upon the minister as a nucleus, and the body politic crystallized upon the church, it is foreign to my purpose to inquire. From historical facts and from the declarations of Hubbard, the historian, and of Governor Winthrop, there is abundant evidence that each town "intended a peculiar government," under which it should be ruled only by its own local laws, and not by any foreign laws. (See vol. I. p. 110, *New Haven Colony Records*).

But there were also three other towns, namely: *Tetoket* or Branford, *Rippowams* or Stamford, *Yenycott* or Southold, whose condition was not that of independent towns governed by their own local laws; but were subject, in part, to the town of New-Haven. It appears that this latter town, New-Haven, possessing comparative wealth, purchased of the Indians the territory on which these several towns were settled, and sold it to the prospective settlers, on terms which made each of these several towns dependent on New Haven in civil matters; though the several churches were entirely independent. In the case of Branford, the contract made with Samuel Eaton, not being carried out, was replaced by one with Samuel Swayne and others. The settlement did not take place until 1644, when the towns had combined in the colony. In the case of Stamford, in the contract made with Robert Coe and others, of Wethersfield, 1640, is the following provision: "that they join in all points with this plantation [New Haven] in the form of government here settled, according to the agreement betwixt this court and Mr. Samuel Eaton about the plantation at Tetoket." The relations of Southold to New Haven were much as those indicated by the contract with Branford and Stamford. It is evident that these three towns never enjoyed the full liberty of making their own local laws, limited as they were, first by their contract with the town of New Haven, and then by the jurisdiction of the colony of New Haven. Thus in 1642, "Goodman Warde of Stamford was in the town of New Haven chosen constable for Stamford this ensuing year." (*N. H. C. R.* vol. I. p. 78.) The relations of these three towns to that of New Haven were, in purpose or fact, partly functional and partly organic; and were somewhat like those of patron and client: they being subject to New Haven, but in part governed by their own local laws. Their history shows that they placed a high value on the right to make their local laws; and had no disturbing force come in, it is probable that, instead of being satellites of New Haven, they would have claimed and enjoyed entire independence in civil as well as ecclesiastical concerns. At least, sufficient evidence is forth-coming that, in each town, there was great dissatisfaction with a subordinate condition in which they were not allowed to make their own laws.

The same Towns in Combination.

But if the three leading towns had indulged a dream of single blessedness, in which they expected to enjoy all the advantages set forth by Plato in his ideal Republic, or by Sir Thomas More in his Utopia, that dream was destined to be disturbed by the formation of the Confederacy of the United Colonies of New England in 1643. These towns could not enjoy the advantages of this confederation unless they themselves should previously combine or confederate under one jurisdiction that could act for the whole. And they could not thus combine under one jurisdiction without practically delegating a portion of that autonomy or self-government in which they each had rejoiced. The caption of the articles of confederation indicates the relations sustained by the towns to each other: "Articles of confederation betwixt the plantations under the government of Massachusetts, the plantations under the Government of New Plymouth, the plantations under the Government of Connecticut, and the Government of New-Haven with the plantations in combination with it." This phraseology was adopted by a kind of prolepsis, in anticipation that these towns would combine under one jurisdiction. The articles were adopted in Boston, May 19, 1643; Theophilus Eaton and Thomas Gregson acting for the town of New Haven, and prospectively for the other towns, but without any formal authority from them. The expected combination of the towns took place, or had taken place, October 27, 1643; when the several towns, by deputies, held the first meeting of the general court for the jurisdiction at New Haven. The town of Branford was not yet organized; Southold had joined the combination, but was not present by deputies. In the general court for the jurisdiction of the colony the several towns had an equality; each town, whatever was its population, was represented by two deputies. There was the governor, the deputy governor, and as many magistrates from the several towns as their neccessities required; a secretary, a treasurer, and a marshal. Thus was the organization of the jurisdiction or colony formed, complete in itself. The basis of this organization was agreed upon at this first meeting of the general court. (See *N. H. Col. Records*, vol. I. p. 112.) It would exceed the limits of this paper to state what were the powers delegated by the towns to the jurisdiction or colony, and what were the rights reserved to themselves. The towns only, as such, were represented in the general court. The towns, as integral elements, constituted the jurisdiction, or the colony.

In regard to this combination of the towns into what is called the New Haven colony, I would remark:

First: That it was produced, not by the attraction of the

towns to one another, but by the fear of the Indians or other enemies.

Second: Milford, acting independently, had admitted to the right of suffrage six planters who were not members of the church. An arrangement was therefore made between that town and New Haven, by which these six voters were allowed still to vote in town matters, but not on what pertained to the jurisdiction of the whole colony; to which was annexed the condition that Milford should not thereafter admit any others not members of the church to that right; thus giving up one of its own local laws.

Third: By thus combining to form the jurisdiction of New Haven colony, the towns practically gave up a portion of their power to form their own local laws, and assumed a position subordinate, in some respects, to the jurisdiction of the colony.

With this subordinate position some of the towns were not entirely satisfied. The Rev. E. B. Huntington, in his *History of Stamford*, uses the following language (p. 73): "From the first there seems to have been [in that town] a degree of restiveness among the settlers, in regard to the limited franchise enjoyed under the jurisdiction of New Haven colony. As early as 1644, but a little more than three years after the settlement, this impatience under such restriction showed itself by the secession of a portion of the colony. The Rev. Richard Denton and those who agreed with him decided to try their fortunes under the Dutch government; and accordingly removed and settled at Hemstead, Long Island," where they could be under their own local laws, and where they allowed all the inhabitants to vote, and made it their duty to do so.

Notwithstanding this secession of twenty planters, dissatisfaction with the civil disabilities still continued; as may be seen from the second volume of the *Colony Records*, and from the following extract from Mr. Huntington's *History*, p. 77, namely, a speech by Robert Basset, in town-meeting, addressed to the law officers appointed by the jurisdiction, at New Haven. "Let *us* have *our* votes. There is no justice in your New Haven tyranny." "We have no English laws or rights. We have no liberties. We have no justice here. We are men-asses for fools to ride, and our backs are well nigh broken. You make laws when you please, and what you please, and give what reasons you please. We are bond men and slaves, and there will be no better times for us till our task-masters are well out of the way." This was in the year 1654. "So positive had this dislike of the New Haven administration become in 1653, that a formal protest seems to have been sent from Stamford, with complaints of their rates and other grievances." These difficulties, springing from a strong attachment to the right of making their own local laws, seem to have continued until the dissolution of the New-Haven confederacy, in 1665.

Similar disaffection, springing from the same cause, existed in the minds of some of the planters at Southold, which exposed them to the charge, in the general court at New Haven, of endeavoring "to overturn the fundamental laws of the colony," in order that their own local laws might prevail in the town. Thus the people of Stamford and of Southold showed their attachment to local law in one way, as New Haven, Milford and Guilford did in another.

THE DISSOLUTION OF THE NEW-HAVEN CONFEDERACY.

On the 20th of April, 1662, His Majesty, Charles the Second, granted a charter to Connecticut, including the colony of New Haven. So strong was the opposition in this colony to a union with Connecticut that it was not consummated until May, 11, 1665, more than three years after the date of the charter. This opposition was grounded on the fact that, by being merged in Connecticut, the colony would lose the liberty of making its own local laws.

It is true, that in some of the towns there were those who preferred the laws of Connecticut to those of New Haven colony, as to the right of suffrage, and were thus prepared to secede from the jurisdiction of one colony to that of the other. And it is remarkable that the general court of Connecticut in August, 1663, raised a committee to treat, not with the general court of New Haven, but with the towns, namely: "with their honored friends of New Haven, Milford, Branford and Guilford;" as if they were separate and independent communities, governed only by their own local laws.

In leaving this branch of the subject, it may not be improper to say that the end aimed at by the founders of the towns in the colony of New-Haven was a noble one, whatever may be said of the means employed. If Platò in his ideal Republic, More in his Utopia, Bacon in his projected New Atlantis, Harrington in his Oceana, and Berkeley in his Gaudentio di Lucca, described a more perfect form of government and a higher condition of society than had ever been realized on earth, it need not seem strange that John Davenport in New Haven, Peter Prudden in Milford, Henry Whitfield in Guilford, and Abraham Pierson in Branford, should endeavor actually to create a better civil government and a higher condition of society than the world has ever witnessed. Objections have indeed been made to some of the local laws in the towns or jurisdiction. But it should be remembered that the people made these laws for themselves and those times, and not for us in our times. They supposed that by their fundamental law limiting the right of suffrage to church members, they were to accomplish the same thing, by moral restraints upon the conscience of the voters, that in modern times is accomplished or intended to be accomplished by written constitutions, state or federal. They adopted the wise opinion that there ought to be some limitation to the right of suffrage, and also the opinion, whether wise or unwise, that this limitation should be a moral one.

SAYBROOK.

The following quotation from the half-century sermon of Rev. Mr. Hotchkiss, shows what were the sentiments of the settlers of Saybrook in regard to local law. "It was in the month of November, 1635, that our Pilgrim fathers came and established themselves in Saybrook, for the free enjoyment of civil and religious privileges without involuntary subjection to any sovereign on earth but that of the people, or to any authority but the law of heaven."

TOWNS ON CONNECTICUT RIVER.

The general court of Massachusetts, May 6, 1635, granted "liberty to the inhabitants of Watertown to remove to any place they may think meet to make choice of, provided they shall continue under this government." Strong opposition was felt in that colony, to the proposed emigration to Connecticut, and a reluctant consent was given by the general court which, with the condition annexed, had application to other towns. Accordingly, emigrants from the three towns of Dorchester, Newtown and Watertown, severally, settled in Windsor, Hartford and Wethersfield, and for a time were governed by commissioners appointed by Massachusetts, who held their first meeting at Hartford, April, 1636.

But the inhabitants of those three plantations or towns, after the experience of the government thus provided by Massachusetts, for a little more than a year, set up a government of their own. They preferred local laws of their own enactment, and a government of their own appointment, which went into operation, May 1, 1637, in place of the government of Massachusetts.

Constitution of Connecticut, 1639.

The planters of those three towns met together at Hartford, January 14, 1639, and formed a constitution in which there is no reference to the government of Massachusetts or of Great Britain. It was the constitution of an independent commonwealth, in which the "supreme power" is declared by the sovereign people to be lodged in the general court.

By this act of separating themselves from the government of Massachusetts, and forming themselves into an independent commonwealth, under a written constitution, they, one hundred and thirty-seven years before 1776, practically announced the cardinal doctrine of the Declaration of Independence, that a people have a right to alter or abolish a form of government in which they are dissatisfied, and establish one which seems to them better adapted to promote their safety and happiness. Thus "a secession," as it is called by Graham, in his *Colonial History*, or a revolution, was effected, which Massachusetts, however reluctant, had the prudence and good sense not to resist. Thus the people of Connecticut, without any to molest or to make them afraid, could rejoice in the supremacy of their own local laws. (See *Conn. Col. Records*, vol. II, p. 20).

At the meeting of the general court at Hartford, October 10, 1639, the same year in which the constitution was adopted, the towns were authorized to manage their internal affairs. But now that there might be no mistake on this point as to the extent of their jurisdiction, the deputies of the towns in general court declare that the towns still *have* authority and right to manage their internal affairs by local law. Each town was a body politic from the first, and was independent, except for a little more than a year, when they submitted to be under the jurisdiction or government of Massachusetts. They had got rid of that government; they had adopted a constitution of their own for general purposes; and they now by their deputies, each town having the same number, declared they still enjoyed the preexisting right to manage their internal concerns. This act of the general court defining the local jurisdiction, and securing for each town a local tribunal, is based on the doctrine prevalent in Connecticut for many generations, *that those whom a law, in its operation, is immediately to affect, are better qualified to judge of its expediency, than those who are at a distance.* Thus, as early as 1639, it was well understood that each town as a body politic had certain rights, and was better qualified to take care of what peculiarly concerns itself, than the colonial legislature was, and that the authority of that legislature applied only to what equally affected the towns in common. In this way, the towns of the Connecticut colony combined or confederated, just as the towns of the New Haven colony confederated, under one jurisdiction. (See *Conn. Col. Records*, vol. I. p. 35.)

The New England Confederacy.

In the year 1643 the New England confederacy was formed between Massachusetts, Plymouth, Connecticut, "and the government of New Haven with the plantations in combination with it." "This confederation," in the language of Palfrey, vol. I. p. 630, "was no less than an act of absolute sovereignty on the part of the contracting states." In this compact or constitution, there are twelve articles, in which the colonies declare, that they will henceforth be called by the name of The United Colonies; that the said united colonies do, "for themselves and their posterities, enter into a firm and perpetual league;" that each colony shall have a peculiar jurisdiction, and that the plantations under the government of each colony shall be forever under that government, with a right to manage its internal concerns in its own way, without the intrusion of others; that each colony raise its quota of men and money for service in war, in its own way, and grant such exemptions as it judges proper; that each colony shall have a right to the rendition of fugitive slaves and apprentices; thus having its own local laws sustained. Of this constitution Bancroft remarks: "To each colony its respective local jurisdiction was carefully reserved. The question of state-rights is nearly two hundred years old." This remark was published in 1842. It is now two hundred and thirty years old.

The plan of this confederacy was adopted in about five years after it was first proposed. This long delay was caused by "divers differences" between Massachusetts and Connecticut. One of these differences is found in the fact that Massachusetts insisted on having a "preeminence," while Connecticut insisted on enjoying a full equality. Winthrop, vol. I. p. 342, A.D. 1638, gives the following account of the matter: "The differences between us and those of Connecticut were divers; but the ground of all was their shyness of coming under our government, which, though we never intended to make them subordinate to us, yet they were very jealous, and therefore, in the articles of confederation, which we propounded to them, and whereby order was taken, that all differences which might fall out, should be ended by a way of peace, and never come to a necessity of danger and force — they did so alter the chief article as all would come to nothing. For whereas the chief article was, that, upon any matter of difference, two, three or more commissioners of every of the confederate colonies should assemble, and have absolute power (the greater number of them) to determine the matter — they would have them only to meet, and if they could agree, so; if not, then to report to their several colonies, and to return with their advice, and so to go on till the matter might be agreed, which besides it would have been infinitely tedious, and extreme chargeable, it would never have attained the end, for it was very unlikely that all the churches in all the plantations would ever have accorded upon the same."

In a letter written the same year, 1638, by Rev. Thomas Hooker, of Hartford, to Governor Winthrop (see vol. I. of *Collections of Connecticut Historical Society*), we have the following passage: "That in the matter which is referred to the judge, the sentence should lie in his breast or be left to his discretion, according to which he should go, I am afraid it is a course which wants both safety and warrant. I must confess, I ever looked at it as a way which leads directly to tyranny, and so to confusion, and must plainly profess, if it was in my liberty, I should choose neither to live nor leave my posterity under such a government."

From these two passages we may understand another difference between Massachusetts and Connecticut. The one, speaking by Winthrop, wished the confederacy or commissioners to have the absolute power of decision; the other, speaking by Hooker, wished the general court of each colony to have the absolute power of decision. The one wished to have absolute power delegated to the confederacy; the other wished to have the absolute power reserved to each colony, and to have Connecticut, in the last resort, governed by its local laws.

The Two Colonies United.

Mention has already been made of the charter granted by Charles II, on the 23d of April, 1662, which virtually merged the colony of New Haven in that of Connecticut; abolishing the laws of the former and substituting those of the latter. This charter, by itself considered, was a liberal one. In the language of Bancroft, "It conferred on the colonists unqualified power to govern themselves. They were allowed to elect their own officers, enact their own laws, administer justice without appeal to England, to inflict punishment, to confer pardons, and, in a word, to exercise every power deliberative and active. The king, far from reserving a negative on the acts of the colony, did not even require that the laws should be submitted to his inspection, and no provision was made for the interference of the English in any case whatever. Connecticut was independent, except in name."

It should be added that the colonists entertained a confiding, generous and affectionate attachment to the king; but they did not recognize any authority in parliament to interfere with their local laws. They insisted on the supremacy of the local laws of the colony in opposition to the imperial laws of parliament. They claimed that they themselves were better qualified to pass laws for their own advantage, living as they did on the territory, than was a parliament at the distance of three thousand miles.

The colony of New Haven, though entertaining these sentiments towards the king, were still strongly opposed to the charter which brought them under the laws enacted by Connecticut. They felt great repugnance to losing not only their local laws but their separate existence, as a body politic. True it is that a certain portion of the people in Stamford, in Southold, in Guilford and Milford, increasing in numbers in the three years or more of delay, preferred the laws and jurisdiction of Connecticut to those of New Haven, and were ready to secede from the one colony to the other. But Mr. John Davenport, of New Haven, and Mr. Abraham Pierson, of Branford, were the true exponents of the sentiments prevailing in the colony, both of whom left the colony in disgust, when its local laws were abolished by the charter of 1662; the one going to Boston; the other taking with him to Newark, New Jersey, his church and others from the towns of Milford and Guilford. They sought exile when they could no longer be under the local laws of the colony of New Haven. They were both martyrs to their love of local self-government; but they were both cheered internally by the *mens conscia recti*, and externally, the one by the voices of his congregation who went with him to the banks of the Passaic, and there laid the foundations of a great city, and the other by the farewell voices of one congregation and the welcoming voices of another congregation in that great city where stood the cradle of liberty.

Diverse Views of the Charter.

The Crown viewed the charters of the colonies as constituting corporations which might be annulled at pleasure, like other corporations in England, which were created as business corporations. The style "Governor and Company" did not imply political power in England.

But the "Freemen" of Connecticut viewed their charter as a solemn compact between them and the king, which could not be altered either by the king or parliament without their consent. The only limitation to the legislative power, conferred by the charter, was that the laws should not be repugnant to the laws of the realm of England. And by the laws of the realm, the colonists understood the constitution, the *fundamental laws*, which are the birth-right of every British subject, secured by *Magna Charta* and *declared in the Bill of Rights.*

The Writ Quo-Warranto issued.

In 1685, soon after the accession of James II, to the throne, and twenty-three years after the grant of the charter, the writ *quo-warranto* was issued against the colony, followed, not long after, by two other writs,[1] in which Connecticut was summoned to show by what right she exercised certain powers. The object of the three writs was to deprive the colony of its charter, and in this way to abolish its local laws. We are told by Trumbull, vol. I, p. 367, that the Assembly, after the most serious deliberation, addressed a letter, in the most suppliant terms, to his majesty, beseeching him to pardon their faults of government, and continue them a distinct colony, in the enjoyment of their civil and religious privileges. "They pleaded the charter they had received from his royal brother, and his commendation of them for their loyalty, in his gracious letters, and his assurances of the continuance of their civil and religious rights." To enforce the reasoning in the letter, they sent William Whiting, of Hartford, to present their petition to the king. Fear and trembling pervaded the assembly and the colony, in view of the apprehended loss of the charter, the basis of its local laws.

Sir Edmund Andros.

In the year 1675, when the Colony was engaged in a war against Philip, Sir Edmund Andros, commissioned by the Duke of York, the patentee of New York, brought forward a claim to all that part of Connecticut which lies west of Connecticut river, and, backed by a strong naval force, demanded the surrender of the fort at Saybrook. Forthwith the assembly, being in session in Hartford, drew up a strong protest against this demand of Major Andros, which with a letter of instructions they sent by express to Captain Thomas Bull, who was in command at Saybrook. How bravely he bore himself in resisting the demand; how he silenced the secretary who attempted to read a paper containing the assumed authority; and how he won from the Major the doubtful compliment of a pun upon his name — "it is a pity that your horns are not tipped with silver"— is familiar to every intelligent school-boy.

On the 31st of October, 1687, Sir Edmund Andros, having been appointed, by the crown, governor of New England, entered Hartford attended by several members of his council, surrounded by a body-guard of sixty men, to take possession of the charter, which, though declared to be forfeited, the assembly had hitherto refused to deliver up.

Of the solemn and protracted debate which took place in the presence of the royal governor, who had declared that the charter was forfeited and the government under it was dissolved; of the extinguishment of the lights, and of the silent and secret conveyance of the charter to the hollow oak, it is not necessary to speak. Nor is it necessary to describe how the governor abolished some of the local laws, and declared that the Indian deeds by which the colonists acquired their lands, were no better than the "scratch of a bear's paw;" how he interfered with town-meetings, and marriages; how he denied the privilege of the writ of *habeas corpus*, under the plea of necessity; how the people endured the loss of their civil liberty nineteen months, when the revolution brought William and Mary to the throne of England, it is not necessary to speak. In 1689, the colony resumed the functions of a free, independent and sovereign commonwealth, subject only to their own local laws.

The Militia.

In the year 1692, Col. Benjamin Fletcher, governor of New York, received a commission from the British government, by which he was invested with plenary power for commanding the militia of Connecticut. As by the charter the right of commanding the militia was expressly given to the colony, the colonial legislature refused to submit to the requisition. On the 26th of October, Governor Fletcher came to Hartford while the assembly was in session, and, in his majesty's name, demanded the submission of the militia to his command, as they would answer it to his majesty, and that they would give him a speedy reply, in two words, "*yes* or *no*." But the assembly boldly refused to surrender their chartered rights, intimating that the demand was subversive of their essential privileges. Among other things they state, "that whoever commanded the persons in a colony would also command the purse, and be the governor of the colony; that there was such a connection between the civil authority, and the command of the militia, that the one could not subsist without the other." The Assembly were willing to *grant* to the king's officer such a portion of the militia, as they should judge proper, but they were not willing that he should take any or all at his discretion. They insisted upon the right to judge what number, and what persons, should be employed in the military service, and to select their officers.

They were not willing to place the people under a military conscription to be enforced by the king's authority. They insisted on the supremacy of their own local laws.

Distribution of Intestate Estates.

From its first organization to the 25th of February, 1728, the Colony had enjoyed the right to settle intestate estates according to its own laws, which differed, in certain important respects, from the laws of England. At that time, namely 1728, the king and council, on the petition of John Winthrop, the grandson of the first Governor Winthrop, of Connecticut, passed a decree annulling the judgment of the superior court, and the probate court, and declaring the colony law, entitled "An Act for the settlement of intestate estates," to be null and void, and of no force or effect whatever, being contrary to the laws of England, and not warranted by the charter of the colony. The governor and company were "to take notice of his Royal Majesty's pleasure hereby signified, and yield due obedience to every particular part thereof, as they should answer the contrary at their peril."

This decree was a blow aimed at the independence and chartered rights of the colony which would open a flood of litigation growing out of the settlement of intestate estates for nearly a century. A special session of the assembly was immediately called, at which their agent in London was instructed to present a petition for the "reversal of the decree, and the reëstablishment of the colony law of descent." In two articles prepared by Hon. J. Hammond Trumbull, when secretary of state, and published in a Hartford newspaper, there is a full and interesting account of the efforts put forth by the colony in defence of its local laws. He quotes Bancroft as saying: "Connecticut so united prudence with patriotism, that successive British ministers were compelled to delay abrogating the charter for want of a plausible excuse." Afterwards he remarks, "the contest with the throne was by no means to be abandoned; but it must be conducted with caution and no vantage-ground given to the enemies of the colony at home or abroad." After a cautious contest with the crown, eighteen years, during a portion at least of which period no intestate estates were settled, in 1726 the colony law of descent of estates "was virtually reëstablished by the court of last appeal in England with the assent of the legal advisers of the crown." Thus the colony again triumphantly vindicated the supremacy of its own local laws.

Plan of Union, 1754.

In June, 1754, at the recommendation of the British ministry, commissioners appointed by Massachusetts, New Hampshire, Rhode Island, Connecticut, New York, Pennsylvania and Maryland, assembled at Albany, for the purpose of forming a plan of union. Such a plan was drawn up by Dr. Franklin, and advocated with his great address, and received the assent of all the commissioners except those of Connecticut, who were strenuously opposed to the extensive powers granted to the president-general, who was to be appointed by the crown. The following statement of the matter is from Pitkin's *History*, vol. II, p. 145.

"The people of Connecticut, in particular, had too long been accustomed to make their own laws, independent of royal authority, to approve of the veto of the president-general. They declared that this might bring his majesty's interest in danger; that officer, in so extensive a territory, not well understanding, or carefully pursuing proper methods for the country's good, all might be ruined before relief could be had from the throne, and that the council, from the respective colonies, were most likely to understand the true interest and weal of the people." They considered, also, the power to levy taxes through so extensive a territory, vested in the president and council, as against the privileges and rights of Englishmen; and that such an innovation in charter-privileges would discourage the industry of the inhabitants, who were jealous of their rights."

"The assembly not only refused to apply to parliament for an act confirming this plan, but instructed their agent to oppose any such act if applied for by the other colonies."

This plan was not adopted. In opposing it, Connecticut was true to herself and her traditions. She was determined to remain, a free sovereign and independent commonwealth governed by her own local laws.

THE CONVENTION OF 1765.

In June, 1765, a convention of commissioners from the colonies met together for consultation in regard to the condition of the colonies under the oppressive acts of parliament. This convention having resolved that each colony should have one voice only, on questions that might arise, among other acts, prepared an address to the king, and a petition to both houses in parliament. The address was drawn by William S. Johnson, one of the most distinguished sons of Connecticut. In this they say:

"Our connection with this empire we esteem our greatest happiness, and security, and humbly conceive it may be so established by your royal wisdom as to endure to the latest period of time. This, with the most humble submission to your majesty, will be most effectually accomplished, by fixing the pillars thereof on liberty and justice, and securing the inherent rights and liberties of your subjects upon the principles of the English constitution."

"In this constitution these two principles are essential, the right of your faithful subjects freely to grant to your majesty such aids, as are required for the support of your government over them, and for other public exigencies; and trial by their peers. By the one they are freed from unreasonable impositions, and by the other from the arbitrary decisions of executive power."

The legislature of Connecticut, in their instructions to their agent in London, after declaring the laying of internal duties to be an infringement of the essential liberties of the colonies, proceeded to say: "We can by no means be content that you should give up the matter of right, but must beg that you would on proper occasion claim and firmly insist on the exclusive right of the colonies to tax themselves, and the privilege of trial by jury; and to maintain these principles in the most effectual manner possible, as what we never can recede from."— *Colony Records.* Thus Connecticut, before the British throne, took strong ground in defence of local law, in opposition to imperial law.

But as parliament still continued to carry into exercise laws which were tyranical and oppressive, a special assembly was called in Connecticut on the 14th of June, 1776, and by a unanimous vote the delegates of the colony in congress was instructed to give "their assent to a declaration of independence, and to unite in measures for forming foreign alliances, and promoting a plan of reunion among the colonies." Thus Connecticut virtually declared her independence, twenty days before the 4th of July. More than a year before this, namely, in 1775, an enterprise was planned in Connecticut to take Ticonderoga by surprise, and to secure the military stores at that place for the benefit of the colonies, and was immediately carried into execution. The party for that purpose was headed by Ethan Allen, a native of Connecticut, who captured the fort.

It should also be borne in mind that the whole subject of the value of local laws as compared with laws of parliament was brought before the towns in Connecticut, those smaller circles of power, for their action, which in many, if not in all cases, was in harmony with the action of the colonial legislature. The town of Boston acted on the subject in Faneuil Hall, as early as the 20th of November, 1772, and then sent out to the other towns, in that colony, a statement of their "rights as men, as Christians, and as subjects." This statement, drawn up by James Otis and supported by Samuel Adams, containing a distinct annunciation of the fundamental principles of the American revolution, was a guiding light to other towns in that colony and in Connecticut, which afterwards held meetings. It was the burning zeal for liberty in the small republics, the towns, that kindled up the fires of the revolution in Connecticut.

Articles of the Old Confederation, 1777.

On the 15th of November, 1777, congress, acting by states, proposed a plan of confederation or union between the states, in which the title of the confederacy was, "The United States of America." In this confederacy, "each state retains its sovereignty, freedom and independence, and every power, jurisdiction and right which is not by this confederation expressly delegated to the United States in congress assembled," where each state had one vote.

When this constitution, or confederation, or league, was brought before the legislature of Connecticut for adoption, that body proposed two amendments, one of which was designed to limit still more the power of the general government, in relation to a standing army, namely, "provided that no standing army shall be kept up by the United States in time of peace, nor any officer or any pensioner be kept in pay by them, who are not in actual service, except such as are or may be rendered unable to support themselves, by wounds received in battle in the service of the said states, agreeably to provisions already made by a resolution of congress."

In May, 1781, Pelatiah Webster, and, in the winter of 1784–5, Noah Webster, citizens of Connecticut, the former residing in Philadelphia, proposed a revision of the federal constitution. A convention of delegates for doing this, met in Philadelphia, May 14, 1787.

Articles of the New Confederation in 1787.

From the debates in the congress, Feb. 21, 1786, it appears that Connecticut, in that body, was opposed, from the first to the last, to the resolution in favor of the appointment by states of delegates to a federal convention. Dr. Johnson, the member of congress, regarded this resolution as "a deadly blow to the existing confederation." The legislature of Connecticut was not forward in appointing delegates to the convention, and the delegates were not forward in their attendance. The day appointed for the meeting was May 14. The meeting did not take place, and the convention was not organized until May 25, when Connecticut by her delegation was not present. One of the delegation was present on the 28th, another appeared on the 30th, and the third on the 2d of June. These three — William S. Johnson, Oliver Ellsworth, and Roger Sherman — the first, by his great learning and logical accuracy, the second, by his legal knowledge and persuasive eloquence, and the third, by his unsurpassed sagacity, exerted great influence in the convention in favor of local law, in opposition to federal law. While a part of the states were in favor of delegating large powers, amounting almost to consolidation, to the proposed government, Connecticut, by her delegates, was in favor of reserving large rights to the states; as may be seen in the published debates.

Thus, June 29, Dr. William S. Johnson, at the moment when the differences in the convention appeared to be irreconcilable, spoke as follows:

"The controversy must be endless whilst gentlemen differ in the grounds of their argument; those on the one side considering the states as districts of people composing one political society, those on the other considering them as so many political societies. The fact is, the states do exist as political societies, and a government is to be formed for them in their political capacity, as well as for the individuals composing them. Does it not seem to follow, that if the states as such are to exist, they must be armed with some power of self defence?"

June 30th, Mr. Ellsworth spoke as follows:

"Under a national government, we should participate in the national security, as remarked by Mr. King; but that was all. What he wanted was domestic happiness. The national government could not descend to the local objects upon which this depended. It could only embrace objects of a general nature. He turned his eyes, therefore, for the preservation of his rights to the state government. From these alone he could derive the greatest happiness he expected in this life. His happiness depended as much upon their existence as a new-born infant on his mother for nourishment. If this reason was not satisfactory, he had nothing to add that could be so."

On June 6th, Mr. Sherman said:

"The objects of the union he thought were few. First, defence against foreign danger; secondly, against internal disputes, and a resort to force; thirdly, treaties with foreign nations; fourthly, regulating foreign commerce, and drawing a revenue from it. These, and perhaps a few lesser objects, rendered a confederation of the states necessary. All other matters, civil and criminal, would be much better in the hands of the states. The people are more happy in small than in large states."

Thus he, too, was opposed to consolidation, and in favor of local law.

On all the great questions involving the amount of rights to be reserved to the states, the delegates of Connecticut were united in favor of the local laws of the state rather than of the federal laws of the United States. Indeed, from the tone of the debates, June 15, it appears that they were distinctly in favor of the principle of the confederation, and opposed to a national government; though they wished a few new powers to be added to those already exercised by the confederation.

On June 22d, Mr. Ellsworth moved that the rule of suffrage in the senate be the same as that established by the articles of confederation, which gave to the states, whether large or small, one vote. On this motion, thus made by Connecticut, the convention was equally divided. July the 2d, Abraham Baldwin, born in Connecticut and educated at Yale college, but now a citizen of Georgia, voted for Mr. Ellsworth's motion, and thus neutralized the vote of that state. Thus the motion was saved for further action, and through the influence of its supporters, under the leadership of Connecticut, became in substance a part of the federal constitution.

August 16th on the motion to strike out from the proposed constitution, the words "and emit bills of credit," Mr. Ellsworth said: "This is a favorable moment to shut and bar the door against paper money. * * * By withdrawing the power from the new government, more friends of influence would be gained to it than by any thing else." The delegates from Connecticut voted *aye;* that is, they voted to withhold the power from the government to issue paper money. This they did for the same reason which influenced Virginia to vote *aye*, as stated by Mr. Madison, namely: to "cut off all pretext for a *paper currency*, and particularly for making the bills a *tender* for public or private debts." Thus to Connecticut belongs the merit of being one of the nine states that refused to give power to the congress to emit bills of credit and make them a legal tender.

August 18th, on the subject of the militia, Mr. Ellsworth remarked:

> "The whole authority over the militia ought by no means to be taken away from the states, whose consequence would pine away to nothing, after such a sacrifice of power. He thought the general authority could not sufficiently pervade the union for such purpose, nor could it accommodate itself to the local genius of the people. It must be in vain to ask the states to give the militia out of their hands."

Mr. Sherman "took notice that the states might want the militia for defence against invasion, insurrections, and for enforcing obedience to their laws. They will not give up this point." Thus it proved in the provisions of the federal constitution. The states did not give up this point, but retained the rights over the militia.

These facts are sufficient to show what was the ground taken in the convention by the delegates from Connecticut. John C. Calhoun, himself educated in Connecticut at Yale college, and at the law school at Litchfield, used the following language concerning them in 1847, in the senate of the United States. "That it is mainly owing to the states of Connecticut and New Jersey, that we have a federal instead of a national government, the best government instead of the worst on earth. Who were the men in these states to whom we are indebted for this admirable government? I will name them; their names ought to be engraven on brass and live forever. They were Chief Justice Ellsworth and Roger Sherman of Connecticut, and Judge Patterson of New Jersey. The other states, further south, were blind; they did not see the future. But to the coolness and sagacity of these three men, aided by a few others not so prominent, we owe the present constitution."

Adoption of the New Federal Constitution.

There had been in Connecticut a strong opposition to the formation and adoption of the proposed constitution, on the ground that it interfered with the local laws of the commonwealth. This we know from testimony and recorded facts. Thus Colonel David Humphrey, in a letter to General Washington, dated January 20th, 1787, speaking of "the omission of federal men in the legislature to press the appointment of delegates to the federal convention," says: "the reason was a conviction, that the persons who could be selected were some of the best anti-federal men in the state, who believed, or acted as if they believed, that the powers of congress were already too unlimited." With Connecticut still in his mind, he says: "They have a mortal reluctance to divesting themselves of the smallest amount of independent, separate sovereignties."

In the state convention which met in Hartford, January, 1788, there was not very much discussion in respect to adopting the new federal constitution. The great battle had been fought in the federal convention, and, as it was supposed, had been won by the Connecticut delegation, and those who sympathized with them in their high estimate of local law and the reserved rights of the states and their sovereignty. There were those who apprehended danger from delegating the power over the purse and the sword, to the federal government; but their fears were allayed by the declaration that the *states reserved the concurrent right of taxation*, and that the federal government *had no authority in the constitution to use the sword against the individual states.*[1] The constitution was adopted by a vote of 128 to 40, there being rather more than three-fourths in favor of its adoption.

The people of Connecticut, strongly attached to their local laws from the first, and strongly opposed to a consolidated, national government, were willing to adopt a federal constitution, such as was offered to them. The word "national," on the motion of their delegate, Oliver Ellsworth, had been struck out of the proposed constitution; as had certain offensive provisions of a national character. They were willing to adopt a *federal* constitution, such as Roger Sherman in his letter to John Adams, 1789, described it to be. His words are: "and the government of the United States being federal, and instituted by a number of sovereign states for the better security of their rights, and the advancement of their interests, they may be considered as so many pillars to support it." They were willing to adopt a constitution recommended by William S. Johnson, a staunch supporter of state rights. He must have known what were its provisions, since he, as chairman of the committee on style, reported it to the federal convention in its finished form. They were willing to adopt such a constitution as Pelatiah Webster in October, 1787, and Noah Webster in his various writings and his dictionary, declared the federal constitution to be, namely, a "compact" between the states severally that created it; they reserving to themselves severally all the powers not distinctly delegated to the several branches of the federal government.

[1] See remarks of Oliver Ellsworth, James Madison, Theophilus Parsons, and Alexander Hamilton.—*Sectional Controversy*, pp. 48, 49, 50.

Opposition to Federal Enactments.

As with a royal government while a colony, so with the federal government while a state, Connecticut has, on many occasions, shown herself prompt to assert the value of local law. That vigilance which is ever the price of liberty, she has bestowed on the encroachments of federal authority, which in earlier days she bestowed on the encroachments of British authority.

Thus, when the federal government, in violation of the federal constitution, in April, 1803, purchased the vast territory of Louisiana, to annex it to the United States, that it might have a voice and a vote in the federal legislature, Connecticut with Massachusetts offered the most decided opposition. So far did they carry this opposition that some of their leading men planned, and talked, and wrote in favor of a separation of the states.

So too, when, in December, 1807, the bill laying an embargo was passed in congress, there was violent opposition made to it in Connecticut, both by the people and by representative men.

At a special session of the general assembly in Hartford, on the 23d day of February, 1809, the following was passed:

"After solemn deliberation and advisement thereon" [the embargo] "the general assembly are decided in the opinion, and do resolve, that the acts aforesaid are a permanent system of measures, abandoning undeniable rights; interdicting the exercise of constitutional privileges, and unprecedented in the annals of nations, and do contain provisions for exercising arbitrary powers, grievous to the good people of this state, dangerous to their common liberties, incompatible with the constitution of the United States, and encroaching upon the immunities of this state.

"*Resolved:* That to preserve the union and support the constitution of the United States, it becomes the duty of the legislature of this state, in such a crisis of affairs, vigilantly to watch over and vigorously to maintain the powers not delegated to the United States, but reserved to the states or to the people; and that a due regard to this duty will not permit this assembly to assist or concur in giving effect to the aforesaid constitutional act passed to enforce the embargo.

"*Resolved:* That this assembly highly approve of the conduct of his excellency the governor [Trumbull,] in declining to designate persons to carry into effect by the aid of the military power, the act of the United States, enforcing the embargo — and that his letter addressed to the secretary of the department of war, containing his refusal to make such designation, be recorded in the public records as an example to persons who may hold places of distinguished trust in this free and independent republic."

On this occasion, an address to the people of the state was issued by the general assembly, in which they speak of themselves as "the guardians of the rights reserved to the states," and say that it is the duty of the legislature to guard the sovereignty of the state.

On the 18th of June, 1812, the federal government declared war against Great Britain. In August the general assembly, at their special session, adopted the report of a joint committee of both houses, of which Calvin Goddard was chairman, in which are the following declarations:

"But it must not be forgotten that the state of Connecticut is a FREE, SOVEREIGN, and INDEPENDENT state; that the United States are a *confederacy of states;* that we are a confederated and not a consolidated republic. The governor of this state is under as high and as solemn an obligation to maintain the lawful rights and privileges thereof, as a free, sovereign, and independent state, as he is to support the constitution of the United States, and the obligation to support the latter imposes an additional obligation to support the former."

The governor's official oath referred to in that report, was the same that had been presented to that officer from the time of the adoption of the federal constitution until 1818, and was as follows: "You, now chosen to be governor over this state of Connecticut, for this year ensuing, and until a new one be chosen, and sworn, do swear by the Ever-living God, to promote the public good and peace of the same, according to the best of your skill; and that you will maintain the lawful rights and privileges thereof, as a *sovereign*, *free*, and *independent* state; also that all wholesome law and orders that are, and shall be made by lawful authority here established, be duly executed; and will further the execution of justice for the time aforesaid, according to the rules of God's word and the laws of this state, *so help you God.*"

In the October session of 1814, the assembly took into consideration a plan that had been submitted to congress by the secretary of war, for filling up the regular army, which placed the militia and the troops raised for the defence of the state at the disposal of the general government. "By the principles of the proposed plan," the assembly say, "our sons, our brothers, and friends are made liable to be delivered, against their will and by force, to the marshals and recruiting officers of the United States, to be employed not for our defence but for the conquest of Canada, or upon any foreign service which the administration might choose to send them." They further declare that plan to be "not only intolerably oppressive, but subversive of the rights and liberties of the state, and the freedom, sovereignty, and independence of the same, and inconsistent with the principles of the constitution of the United States."

The Governor of Connecticut took the ground that, by the constitution of the United States, the entire control of the militia is given to the state, except in certain specified cases, namely: to execute the laws of the union, to suppress insurrections, and to repel invasions, and he contended that neither of these cases actually existed. He also took the ground that the militia could not be compelled to serve under any other than their own officers, with the exception of the president himself, when personally in the field. For both of these reasons he refused to comply with the requisition of General Dearborn.

Accordingly, at the session of the general assembly in August, the following resolution was passed:

"*Resolved*, That the conduct of his excellency the governor in refusing to order the militia of the state into the service of the United States, on the requisition of the secretary of war, and Major-General Dearborn, meets with the entire approbation of the assembly."

The course pursued by Connecticut in support of the reserved rights of the states against the usurpation of the federal government was justified by a similar course pursued by Massachusetts, sanctioned by the declared opinion of the supreme court of that state.

What was the reason that Connecticut thus refused to place the militia under the officers of the federal government? The reason was substantially the same as that which, in 1692, influenced Connecticut to refuse to place the militia under the officers of the British government. She respected in the one case the lawful authority of the British government, and in the other the lawful authority of the federal government, but in neither case would she submit to unconstitutional requisitions. The rights granted in the one case, and the rights reserved in the other, were the foundation of local laws. She valued her local laws too highly to surrender her granted rights in 1692, to Col. Fletcher, or her reserved rights in 1812, to General Dearborn.

In January, 1815, at a special session, an act was passed to secure the rights of parents, guardians and masters. The following is the first section of the act:

"*Be it declared and enacted by the governor and council, and house of representatives in general court assembled.*

"That the power assumed by congress of removing the legal disabilities of minors to make contracts, and investing them with that capacity in order to enlist at pleasure into the army of the United States, and thereby annul the most important relations in society, is repugnant to the spirit of the constitution of the United States, and an unauthorized interference with the laws and rights of this state." In section second, a penalty of five hundred dollars or imprisonment for one year is affixed to the crime of pursuading a minor to depart from the state with the intention of enlisting in the army of the United States. In section third, a penalty of five hundred dollars is affixed to the crime of enticing or causing one to be enlisted in the army of the United States, with the knowledge that he is a minor.

In the autumn of 1814, the general assembly of Connecticut, while in session, received a communication from the general assembly of Massachusetts, containing a proposal to unite with Massachusetts, Rhode Island and other states, in convention, to deliberate on the dangers which beset them, and "to devise, if practicable, means of security and defence, which may be consistent with the preservation of their resources from total ruin, and adapted to their local situation, mutual relations and habits, and not repugnant to their obligations as members of the union." The communication was referred to a committee, and their report was adopted by the legislature. Seven delegates were appointed to represent the state in the convention, which was appointed to be held in Hartford, December 15th, 1814. After a session of about three weeks, the convention made a report, containing a statement of their views and the proposal of seven amendments to the federal constitution.

What were the grievances of which Connecticut complained? They may all be resolved into these two: First, that the federal constitution, in the actual working of some of its parts, was injurious to her local interests. Second, that the federal government had usurped powers not delegated in the constitution. What was the proposed remedy for these grievances? The seven proposed amendments to the federal constitution. These, it was supposed, would correct the workings of the federal constitution, by which the local interests of the state were injured and prevent the usurpations of the federal government, by which their local rights were endangered and their local laws weakened.

CONNECTICUT WORTHIES.

And who were the leading men in Connecticut who took ground against unconstitutional encroachments upon state rights, in 1804, 1807, and 1814? They were JONATHAN TRUMBULL, ROGER GRISWOLD, JOHN COTTON SMITH, JAMES HILLHOUSE, CHAUNCEY GOODRICH, DAVID DAGGETT, CALVIN GODDARD, ROGER MINOT SHERMAN, and others like them. These men were familiarly acquainted with the circumstances under which the federal constitution was formed, its true meaning in relation to delegated powers and reserved rights; were acquainted personally, more or less intimately with WILLIAM S. JOHNSON, OLIVER ELLSWORTH, the first of whom was still living, were sustained by the highest authorities in Massachusetts, among whom was Chief Justice THEOPHILUS PARSONS, men who had not failed to understand the federal constitution. These eminent men knew that Connecticut is a *free*, *sovereign*, and *independent state*, and that as a party to the compact of the federal constitution, she knew what powers she had delegated, and what rights she had reserved, and that she was under as much obligation to preserve her reserved rights from the encroachments of the federal authorities, as she was to accord to those authorities the free exercise of all the powers delegated to the federal government. As one of the high contracting parties to the compact of the constitution, the federal treaty between the states, she must judge of any infractions of the federal treaty and "the mode and measure of redress."

Respect for the Local Law of Other States.

And the people of Connecticut showed a generous regard for the local laws of other states made in conformity with the right reserved to them by the federal constitution. On September 11th, 1835, "in pursuance of a call for a public meeting by the mayor and council of New Haven, to take into consideration the Report and Resolutions of the city of Charleston, South Carolina, August 10th, 1835, which was sent to each incorporated city and town in the United States; the citizens express their opinions in regard to certain societies and individuals who have circulated incendiary publications through some of the southern states contrary to the laws, and against the peace of the United States.

1. *Resolved*, That the constitution of the United States in which the different and delicate interest of the *sovereign states* were compromised and settled, etc.

3. *Resolved*, in the language of a report of a committee of the whole house of representatives made in 1790, in the second session of the first congress which assembled under the constitution and by that body ordered to be entered on the journal, "That congress have no authority to interfere in the emancipation of slaves or in the treatment of them in the different states, it remaining with the several states alone to provide any regulations therein which humane and true policy may require.

"Henry W. Edwards, president,
Noah Webster and David Daggett, vice presidents.

That first abolition firebrand was not thrown into congress from Connecticut. In a letter written at the time by Governor Oliver Wolcott of Litchfield to his son, afterwards Governor Oliver Wolcott is the following, "I wish that congress would prefer the white people of this country to the black. After they have taken care of the former, they may amuse themselves with the other people."

The present writer was at the time, 1835, informed that the ground taken by one of the speakers at least, at the New Haven meeting was that the course pursued by the abolition societies was contrary to the principles of *international law* which obtains between the states, they being regarded as so many nations, or republics.

A public meeting of the citizens of Hartford held September 26th 1835, in full accord with the citizens of New Haven adopted the following language, "Whereas certain persons in the Middle and Eastern states have formed associations for the avowed purpose of effecting the abolition of slavery in the other states, and in pursuance of said design, have established a press from which they issued several newspapers and periodicals devoted to the aforesaid objects, and filled with the most inflammatory matter, whereby the *confederacy is endangered.*

3. *Resolved*, That the states, in confederating, retained all rights as independent sovereignties, except such as were expressly delegated to the Union."

ISAAC TOUCEY, president,
ELISHA PHELPS, JOSEPH PLATT, vice presidents.

The voices of the two leading cities spoke the general sentiment of Connecticut at that time.

She loved her own local laws and she was ready to discountenance any interference with the local laws of other states.

NULLIFICATION BY CONNECTICUT.

In 1838, the legislature of Connecticut passed an act nullifying in part the act of congress of 1793, for the restoration of the fugitive slaves. The act of congress provided that "When a person held to labor in any of the United States, or in either of the teritories north, west, or south of the river Ohio, under the laws shall escape into any other of the said states or territories, the person to whom such labor or service is due, or his attorney, is hereby empowered to seize or arrest such fugitive from labor, and to take him or her before any magistrate of county, city or town corporate wherever such seizure or arrest may be made, and upon proof to the satisfaction of said judge or magistrate, by oral testimony or affidavit taken before and certified by a magistrate of any such state or territory, that the person so seized or arrested, doth under the laws of the state or terri-

13

tory from which he or she fled, owe service or labor to the person claiming him or her, it shall be the duty of such judge or magistrate to give a certificate thereof to said claimant, his agent or attorney, which shall be sufficient warrant for removing said fugitive from service or labor to the state or territory from which he or she had fled." The law from which this is an extract, was passed in 1793, and bears the approval of George Washington, president.

In the face of this act of congress, the Connecticut legislature, in the eighth section of her nullifying enactment, declares, "that any justice of the peace or other officer violating this provision, shall forfeit and pay the party aggrieved five hundred dollars, and shall be deemed guilty of a misdemeanor." This blow by the Connecticut legislature at the George Washington act, nullifying it in part, might have been deemed chivalrous, had it not been struck under the mask of the following title to the bill: "An act for the fulfilment of the obligations of this state imposed by the constitution of the United States in regard to persons held to service or labor in one state escaping into another, and to secure the right of trial by jury in the cases herein mentioned."

In the same spirit the legislature of Connecticut in 1854, passed an act entitled: "An act for the defence of liberty in this state." Under this specious title, the real design was, as declared by its friends in the legislative debates, to *prevent the execution of the fugitive slave law in Connecticut*, namely, the law passed by Congress in 1850.

The following is from the report of the debate in the senate by John B. Carrington Esq., Editor of the "*Journal and Courier*," New Haven.

"Henry B. Harrison of New Haven, who introduced the bill, avowed his belief that it would render the fugitive slave law inoperative in Connecticut. He explained the provisions of the bill, and illustrated its operation, by supposed cases.

"Hon. Mr. Boyd [John Boyd late secretary of state], believed desperate diseases require desperate remedies. He had some faith in the homeopathic remedy, that like requires like, and as he believed the exigences of the time demanded it, he thanked the senator for introducing the bill. Hon. Mr. Sanford [Judge Sanford of the Supreme Court], did not recognize much of the homeopathic principle in this bill; he saw more of the knife and caustic in it: but he did see in it new and important principles which, he believed, were entirely constitutional, and would be so decided by the supreme court. He thought the senator from the 4th deserved much credit for introducing it.

"Hon. Mr. Deming [Henry C. Deming, M.C.], thought the bill, at least in the spirit, conflicted with the constitution of the United States.

"Hon. Mr. Miner [Ex Governor Wm. S. Miner], desired Mr. D. to point out a single line, sentence or word, that was unconstitutional. He was unable to find it.

"Hon. Mr. Sanford again examined at some length, the provisions of the bill. He thought that the south had driven this matter so fast, that it had driven us back to our reserved rights if we had any. He would occupy the last inch the constitution left them, come square up to the line, but not one step over. He would oppose the fugitive slave law by every means in his power, within the limits of the constitution.

"Hon. Mr. Deming said the bill was nicely drawn — its phraseology was adapted to the case — but it was not in equityand justice deserved by our own southern brethren if they behave pretty well.

"Hon. Mr. Boyd, offered Mr. D. as an illustration, if Shylock claims his pound of flesh, he must be careful not to take any of the blood. Same day. Bill prohibiting the use of any court house or jail or other public building, for the trial or confinement of a fugitive slave under a penalty of $1,000. Mr. Boyd moved to amend so as to provide that any building for such a purpose, shall be rased to its foundation, and remain a perpetual ruin. Lost."

In Senate, Tuesday, June 27, 1864.

Personal Liberty bill taken up.

"Mr Sanford addressed the senate with great clearness, dignity, and force, in which he expressed his belief that the bill as amended, was in every respect constitutional, that the emergencies of the times demanded such a law: portrayed the odious features of the fugitive slave law, showing that it was a vain expectation that we should not constitutionally oppose it; examined the provisions of the bill before the senate, as obstructing the progress of the slave catcher, whom he pronounced the most despicable being that ever wore human form."

Analogy between Colony Rights and State Rights.

From the foregoing statements of historical facts, it is seen that colony rights and state rights are substantially the same, and that there are the same reasons for defending state rights, that there were formerly for defending colony rights. Both have had the same foundation, namely, the competency of Connecticut to manage her own internal concerns, without the intrusion of kings and parliament, in the one case, and without the intrusion of presidents and congress in the other. There have been substantially the same safeguards in regard to both classes of rights, namely *magna charta*, and the charter of the colony in the one case, and the federal constitution and the state constitution in the other. There was the same temptation on the part of Great Britain to despoil the colony of its rights, that there has been since to despoil the state of its rights, namely, the *lust of power*.

Human nature has grown no better since James the Second, Sir Edmund Andros and Fletcher, may appear, or have appeared, under other names clothed with federal authority. The minions of the president and of congress, may be just as corrupt and despotic, as those of James or of the long parliament. There was the same temptation on the part of the colony to crook the pregnant hinges of the knee, and yield itself to the lust of power, that there has been since on the part of the state. There was the same insidious pretence of the greater good to Great Britain, that there has sometimes been since of the greater good to the United States, as if this "greater good," could justify the colony in surrendering its chartered rights, or the state in surrendering its reserved rights. There was the same plea of "necessity, the tyrant's plea," to justify the violation of the charter, that there has been to violate the federal constitution, when the necessity was created by the royal authorities in the one case, and by the federal authorities in the other.

When under the first federal constitution adopted in 1781, the people in the several towns were so apprehensive that congress was encroachiug on the rights of state sovereignty that meetings were held to investigate the subject. On the 16th of October, 1783, the town of Hartford gave instructions to their representatives in the general assembly, THOMAS SEYMOUR and GEORGE PITKIN. "In these instructions the representatives were expressly directed strenuously to oppose all encroachments of the American congress on the sovereignty and jurisdiction of the separate states and every assumption of power not expressly vested in them by the confederation. A convention was held in

Middletown, September 1783, in which a majority of the towns were represented, for the purpose of investigating the question whether congress had not exceeded its constitutional powers, in granting a commutation of pay to the officers of the army.

Responsibility of the Governor and the Assembly.

It has been supposed in Connecticut, that the governor and assembly for the time are the constituted guardians of the state; that when there should be any encroachments of the king or parliament on the chartered rights of the colony, or any encroachment of the president or congress on the reserved rights of the state, it would be the sacred duty of the governor and the assembly to interpose for its protection, and with a strong hand resist the encroachments.

And how watchful and faithful some of those ancient governors were! "I will argue that question with your majesty," said one of them in a written communication. They snuffed tyranny in the breeze. And how faithful too were their agents abroad! such men as Sir Henry Ashurst, Fitz John Winthrop, and William S. Johnson. On the 16th of May, 1769, the last mentioned was a spectator in parliament, when Grenville, in the midst of one of his speeches, looked up in the gallery and said, "I hope there are no American agents present; I must hold such language, as I would not have them hear." "I have expressly ordered the sergeant to admit none," said the speaker, "and you may be assured there are none present." Yet Johnson of Connecticut had braved the danger of an arrest, and sat in the gallery to record the incidents of the evening for the warning of his countrymen.

The Ruling Motive.

Does any one ask why Connecticut has taken such a deep interest for the preservation of colony rights and state rights? The cause can be found in the fact that the rights of *every individual* were, or are involved in those rights. Life, liberty, and prosperity are protected by state laws based upon state rights.

The sovereign state of Connecticut is bound to preserve all her reserved rights for the benefit of every *individual citizen* of the commonwealth.

Our houses and our graves, our lands while we hold them and the transmission of them to others, our rights as parents and children, as husbands and wives; our churches and seminaries of learning, all our most valuable interests in our mortal pilgrimage, are protected by state laws, based on our state constitution and that is based on state rights, and not on the powers delegated to the federal government. The federal government was not formed for the promotion of morals, education, or religion. Most appropriately did Oliver Ellsworth, in the constitutional convention, say "that he turned his eyes for the preservation of his rights to the state government. From these alone he could derive the greatest happiness he expected in this life.

Change of State Constitution.

In 1818, the present state constitution replaced the charter constitution. It was followed by some change in the local laws, which were thus brought into harmony with the constitution.

Change of Policy.

Not long afterwards the system of high tariffs was introduced by the federal government, by which certain parts of the country were taxed for the benefit of the manufacturing states, of which Connecticut is one. The assertion of state-rights in opposition to the encroachments of the federal government would not come with as good a grace from Connecticut while that government by tariffs was legislating for her benefit, as it would when the same government by restrictions on commerce was legislating for her injury. The gallant defence of her rights made by Connecticut, for a long period, against usurpations, British or federal, often stimulated by the injuries inflicted by those usurpations upon her material interests, can hardly be expected to be made now against the encroachments of the federal government, inasmuch as the patronage of that government in the shape of tariffs, contracts, and lucrative offices, united with the practical wisdom, inventive genius, and characteristic thrift of her people, have made her, in proportion to the number of her inhabitants, the richest state in the union. It is not necessary for her now to calculate the value of the federal union, as when restrictions were imposed on her commerce. She can leave this to other states which have not been thus benefited by federal legislation and federal patronage. And yet Connecticut has, even in this later period, shown forth her hereditary love of local law, and reserved rights; as, for instance, in the legislation of 1838, and, in the legislation of 1854, as a sovereign state she took extreme ground in opposition to certain federal laws enacted in 1793, and 1850, practically nullifying them.

If it should be asked, how it has happened that Connecticut has, from the first, been the gallant and successful advocate and defender of local law, against centralized and imperial authority, the following is a brief answer, which might be strengthened by historical proof. The immigrant settlers on Long Island sound and the river had felt the oppression of prelatical and parliamentary tyranny to such a degree, that they fled from it to enjoy liberty here, in the establishment of separate independent churches in which local law, the collected will of the members, should prevail free from the canons of the national church. "As ideas govern the world," so they did the puritans of Connecticut. As it was a ruling idea among them that each local church was competent to make its own laws without any foreign control, they easily extended the idea to civil communities. So did others. "No bishop, no king," said James I. That is, the same idea which was producing a revolt from the bishops, would, when carried out, produce a revolt from the king; and thus it proved.

It is true that, for a long period, the people of Connecticut cherished loyalty to the king, in the English sense of the term, and gratitude to him for granting the charter which conferred upon them the privilege of being governed by their local laws. Yet in time even these were withdrawn, when the supremacy of their local laws was threatened.

Thus, in the language of Halleck, one of her sons, Connecticut is

"A vestal state which power could not subdue,
Nor promise win — like her own eagle's nest,
Sacred — the San Marino of the West."

In the foregoing statements it is seen that Connecticut, from her love of local law in church and state has been inclined to independency, and opposed to centralization. She has been willing to confederate, provided large rights are reserved for independent action. Her liberties, religious, and civil, are found in these reserved rights. The churches were independent; but were willing to confederate for certain purposes, as they did, in 1708, on the Saybrook platform. The towns were at first independent; but they were willing in each of the two colonies to confederate, but reserving large rights for separate, independent action. The two colonies in 1643, were willing to confederate with Massachusetts and Plymouth, but they carefully reserved large rights for the independent action of each. Connecticut was willing to confederate in the first union of the states, in 1781, but she reserved large rights for her separate and independent action. She was willing to confederate in the new, or present, federal union of the states, but reserved large rights for her separate, independent and intelligent action as a sovereign state.

We have seen how correctly and successfully Connecticut has struggled to establish and sustain free institutions, and local laws. But instead of claiming the glory for herself, she modestly, in the motto on her armorial bearings ascribes it to God. SUSTINET QUI TRANSTULIT.

www.ingramcontent.com/pod-product-compliance
Lightning Source LLC
LaVergne TN
LVHW021430110826
845150LV00007B/2174

* 9 7 8 1 4 2 5 5 0 6 7 7 3 *